PRACTICAL GUIDE TO
SPECIFIC LEARNING DIFFICULTIES

£3.50.

Practical Guide to

Specific
Learning
Difficulties

JEAN BLIGHT
and
CHRIS STRIANESE COULTON

A practical guide to help people understand
children who are having difficulties with
learning and coping with life.

EGON PUBLISHERS LIMITED
Royston Road
Baldock, Herts SG7 6NW

ISBN 1-904160-84-0

Designed and printed by Streets Printers
Royston Road, Baldock, Hertfordshire SG7 6NW,
England

Published by
Egon Publishers Limited
Royston Road, Baldock, Hertfordshire SG7 6NW,
England

CONTENTS

PREFACE

In 1985 I wrote 'A Practical Guide to Dyslexia', which is a booklet describing the signs and symptoms of dyslexia and practical ways of helping the dyslexic.

After teaching and assessing children for 22 years, my knowledge and understanding of the dyslexic had increased greatly, and I felt it was time to write another book to bring the information up to date.

When I began the work in 1980, the children I saw and assessed seemed to have more easily defined problems than the children I see now.

This may have been a lack of knowledge and understanding learning and behavioural development. However, since 1980, dyspraxia and attention span deficit disorder (hyperactive) have been recognised as possible reasons why children find learning so difficult.

In this book, the signs and symptoms cover dyslexia, dyspraxia, attention span deficit disorder (hyperactive), auditory processing disorder and some signs in the autistic spectrum. Sometimes it is difficult to give a clear definition of the difficulties because they merge into one another. Fortunately, each child has only some symptoms of each disorder.

This book is the result of my teaching and assessing children and is anecdotal; it is what I have observed over the years. So no scientific research has been carried out; it is just experience and intense interest in the children and adults I see. They have been my teachers, and I thank them.

Over the years, I have attended many, many courses, lectures and seminars, and I am still learning. Some of the ideas gained from these experts have been incorporated into my work. The experts who gave these courses need my thanks.

When I began to write this book, I asked my friend, Chris Strianese Coulton to become my co-author. Chris is a teacher and has three very special sons who have had some difficulties. I wanted her input as a parent and it has been a great partnership. Thank you Chris.

At the end of the book, we have compiled information about organisations that help children and adults overcome their difficulties.

This is not a developmental handbook to assess progress and stages of development. It is meant as a broad guide. This information is a starting point for you to begin finding the appropriate help for your child and to explore other possible treatments.

Jean Blight

ACKNOWLEDGEMENTS

We thank all those who have contributed to this book including Dawn Skye and Sarah Roberts. We also thank all those who read the first draft and constructively commented on it, Anita Dalton who patiently typed many of the initial drafts, Richard Webster who edited the book, Andrew Blight who typed the final drafts and David Blight for his help and support.

Finally, we thank our families and especially Andy for their support and encouragement and our children who have taught us so much.

THE AUTHORS

JEAN BLIGHT

Jean Blight is a very experienced teacher who has a son with dyslexia. She has taught in infant and junior schools and a college of further education. She taught in a Special School for ten years and was the head of an assessment unit for two years. Then, in January 1982, she helped to set up the Watford Dyslexia Unit and was the Assistant Director from then until 1985 when she became the Director. During this time, she was a teacher trainer. In April 1990, she was appointed Head of Special Help at Beechwood Park School. She retired in 1998 but continues to assess and teach private pupils. Her book 'Practical Guide to Dyslexia' was published in 1985. She has worked for the Hertfordshire Dyslexia Association for many years and is currently the Vice-President.

CHRIS STRIANESE COULTON

Chris Strianese Coulton received a BA in Child Psychology from Saint Joseph's College, New York, in 1979. Every summer from 1973 to 1978 she was a counsellor in a voluntary youth organisation working closely with large groups of children from diverse backgrounds. She was a supply teacher for the New York City Board of Education and she also spent several years in business. From 1980 to 1981, she worked for Hitachi America Ltd, NY, 1981 to 1986 for Goldman Sachs & Co. NY, and 1987 to 1989 for Fundamental Brokers Inc. in London. Her experiences with her own three sons triggered a keen interest in helping children with special needs.

INTRODUCTION

This book describes the symptoms that children can display if they are having difficulties in learning and retaining information, and it suggests ways of helping such children. It is a basic introductory text to help parents, and others interested, to identify children with special needs such as dyslexia, dyspraxia, autism spectrum disorders and children who need special attention. It is also relevant for children who are not reaching their full potential.

There is a broad spectrum of difficulties, with varying degrees of severity and with symptoms that overlap and make diagnosis difficult. We describe patterns of childhood behaviour, signs and symptoms that should set off alarm bells. This will enable parents to identify the behaviour patterns that may indicate special needs.

We do not pretend there are easy solutions to the problems created by these difficulties. Clearly the difficulties are as individual as each child, and help needs to be individually tailored. The trouble is finding out what help is available. Various therapies may suit individual children at different times in their development. There is help available and hope for the future.

Finding that your child is different from others can be stressful and emotional. It is at that time, that you want information, to know what options are available, so that you can see beyond the early confusion and make more informed choices.

We all dearly love our children and want the best for them. There are times when we worry that things might not be quite right. Therefore, we hope that this book will be a resource that will give you some direction and hope for the future.

Your child might be unusual yet cope well. His minor disabilities might not cause you or him serious problems, and it is great if everyone is happy. In other circumstances, the children and their parents feel uncomfortable with their situations. They may sense unease, stress or frustration, etc. It is in these cases that we aim to help people to re-assess their problems, and perhaps even see that their present difficulties could actually be strengths. Just as we need people who are good at detail, we need people who can see the big picture and can think laterally to solve problems. We need to value unique abilities.

In this world we each choose our own ways. There are many ways to accomplish things. In this text we present positive choices that will enable you to provide some of the skills that your children will need for successful and happy lives. We want you to know that there is help available and hope for their futures

The majority of children with the special needs discussed in this book are boys and to avoid the complexity of using 'he or she', 'his or her' etc. we have chosen to use 'he', 'his', 'him', etc. We acknowledge that there are a significant number of girls who also have these special needs (see the personal stories in the rest of the book).

There are a number of names used to describe the various difficulties a child might have, and not everyone will understand what the names mean. We have included brief definitions of the difficulties referred to in this book below.

DYSLEXIA

Dyslexia is the name given to difficulties in learning to read, comprehend and write. It affects a minority of children who attend ordinary schools and are taught normally and who show no other signs of backwardness. Dyslexia also presents many problems for adults.

DYSCALCULIA

Dyscalculia is the difficulty some people have when working with numbers, their values, order sequences, tables and working out problems.

DYSGRAPHIA

Dysgraphia is the difficulty some people have in writing symbols in an acceptably recognised form.

READING MUSICAL NOTATION

Reading musical notation can cause difficulties. In particular, learning to play the piano can be complicated by having to learn two staves instead of one, as for a string or wind instrument.

DYSPRAXIA

Developmental dyspraxia is an impairment or immaturity of the organisation of movement. It is an immaturity in the way that the brain processes information, which results in messages not being properly or fully transmitted. The term dyspraxia comes from the word praxis, which means 'doing, acting'. Dyspraxia affects the planning of what to do and how to do it. It is associated with problems of perception, language and thought. (Definition taken from the Dyspraxia Foundation website.)

ATTENTION DEFICIT DISORDER (HYPERACTIVE)

Attention Deficit Disorder (Hyperactive) (ADD(H)) is a neurological condition that is usually diagnosed in children but can be found in adults. Hyperactivity, impulsivity and any combination are the main categories of ADD(H). Although ADD(H) begins in childhood, adults can continue to suffer from these disorders as well.

When childlike behaviours continue to show themselves in persistent patterns of hyperactivity, impulsivity or both, and are most severe and more frequent than typically observed, then the child might have ADD(H).

Some of the symptoms of ADD(H) are inattention, being easily distracted, fidgeting, etc., but professional diagnosis is required to confirm the condition.

AUTISTIC SPECTRUM DISORDER

Autistic Spectrum Disorder (ASD) is a pervasive developmental disability that can cause children to have problems with how they learn, communicate, and how they perceive their environment and relate to other people.

Children with ASD have their own individual ways of processing information and understanding the world. However, they vary widely in their range of skills and abilities.

All children have some difficulties in their lives when learning, but if they are coping well with them and have learned some useful skills to help them, then there is no special reason for concern. If, on the other hand, they find it hard to learn and are making little progress, and are becoming frustrated or worried, then it is time to act. It is amazing how much better most children feel when their problems have been sympathetically identified, their problem is given a name, and assistance is offered to alleviate the problem. Often they feel they are to blame for their failure and begin to feel depressed, so early identification is important.

After a child's disorder has been identified, the parents can feel guilty because they had not recognised the symptoms earlier. In many instances, help now is at hand, and parents can move on more positively.

Some parents find it hard to come to terms with the fact their children have learning difficulties, for many personal reasons, but if they can overcome this problem, then great things can happen.

There are some children who have severe learning difficulties and who show symptoms of dyslexia, dyspraxia and ADD(H), but they will require more specialist help that this book sets out to provide.

PARENTS' CONCERNS

At some time or other, all parents have concerns about the development of their children. As a child grows up, there may be numerous problems and difficulties that he faces, and normally he will solve and overcome them. However, when difficulties persist longer than with his peers or cause him to be distressed, it is time to find out if there is a problem that needs professional help.

These are some of the questions and comments that have been asked by concerned parents and might indicate the child has special educational needs. Here are some typical remarks from parents.

'My child is frustrated and miserable, has low self-esteem, and is not achieving what is expected.'

'He has frequent mood-swings, is easily excitable, and readily over-reacts.'

'He finds it difficult to get on with other children, has poor eye contact and inappropriate responses in social situations.'

'He's not interested in what's going on around him and seems to live in his own little world.'

'My child has skipped stages of development such as crawling.'

'He is so clumsy! He keeps bumping into furniture, has terrible trouble with anything that involves using his balance. I still have to help him do up his clothes when he gets dressed.'

'He's always fidgeting, I can't get him to sit still, and he never seems to stand up straight.'

'He is such a messy eater. He is so disorganised and untidy.'

'He finds it difficult to get to sleep and still wets the bed.'

'My child seems to forget very quickly what I've told him.'

'He has problems concentrating on his schoolwork and gets side-tracked easily.'

'He seems to behave very differently when he's at home from how he behaves when he's at school.'

'He seems so tired when he gets back from school.'

'He seems to be hypersensitive to touch, light and noise.'

'He has difficulty coping with sticky or dirty hands.'

He finds some materials almost impossible to wear and finds tags in clothes very irritating.'

'He has food intolerances and allergies.'

'He has problems with reading, spelling and maths and keeps misses linking words such 'as', 'is', 'and', 'not', 'of'.

'He doesn't seem to understand the purpose of reading. It should be for information and enjoyment, shouldn't it?'

'He sometimes has difficulty with reading. Some days he's really good and other days he's really bad.'

'He seems so bright yet his reading and spelling test results are so poor.'

When reading through this list of concerns, you will realise that any child is likely to fit into one or two of the categories. If your child has no other severe difficulties and is coping well with life, then you are very fortunate. If, however, your child has at least four or five symptoms and is experiencing the difficulties with learning we mention, then read on.

SIGNS AND SYMPTOMS

INTRODUCTION

In this chapter of the book, the signs and symptoms of the disorders are presented as they appear at the several stages of development.

In each section, there may be symptoms that are repeated. This presents all of the relevant information for a child in one place to make it easier for parents to refer to. It also gives a clear picture of how these disorders might develop.

It is important to remember that we all have our imperfections, whether it is poor eyesight, hearing, a funny walk, skinny legs or teeth that need braces. Learning difficulties should be accepted as a part of life.

The signs and symptoms of a child with specific educational needs have been grouped into the following age ranges:

0 to 1 year,
1 to 2 years,
2 to 3 years,
3 to 5 years,
5 to 7 years,
7 to 13 years and
13 to 18 years.

The signs and symptoms section for each age group have the following structure.

Sleep

Examples of abnormal sleep related problems, e.g. problems going to sleep, bed-wetting.

Eating

Examples of eating related problems, e.g. food allergies, eating messily.

Motor skills
Examples of motor skill related problems, e.g. the way in which the child moves his body, hands or feet.

Social development
Examples of problems relating to social interactions, e.g. abnormal behaviour with his peers.

Sensitivity
Examples of over-sensitivity to various stimuli, e.g. loud noises, bright lights, and certain types of material or tags on clothes touching his skin.

Speech
Examples of speech-related problems, e.g. he does not always understand verbal instructions and has problems finding the right words when giving answers.

Education problems
Examples of problems that occur at school, e.g. slower than expected progress in reading, writing and spelling.

0–1 YEAR

Sleeping
The child does not settle into a regular pattern of sleep. This might be caused by ear infections, stomach upsets and other medical problems, which may need further investigation.

Eating
The child shows signs of early allergies, intolerance to milk or wheat, and is particular about what he eats.

Motor skills
The child might be late in achieving developmental milestones, such as sitting up. He might skip stages of development such as crawling, which is important for neurological cross pattern development. He shows repetitive movement of arms and legs and never seems to get

comfortable. When frustrated or distressed he may begin to exhibit worrying behaviour such as head banging.

Social development
The child requires the constant attention of adults and finds it difficult to play games such as 'peep-bo' because he does not understand the rules of the game. Or the child is almost too good and is self-contained. He may have inaccurate perceptions of the world and difficulties relating to it. Perhaps he is irritable, clingy or easily distressed.

Sensitivity
The child is unusually sensitive to loud noises and bright light. His skin is sensitive, so that he dislikes close contact, textures of fabrics and labels in clothes. Soap, shampoo and washing powder may cause distress.

Speech
He lacks the early signs of pre-speech, i.e. making consistent sounds for objects and copying new sounds.

1–2 YEARS

Sleep
Difficulties with sleep continue (see 0–1 year).

Eating
Eats messily and prefers to use his fingers. He has trouble with lumps in food and prefers smooth textures. He can develop strong preferences and can be a picky eater.

Motor skills
The child is unsteady on his feet and falls over easily. He still lacks fine motor control particularly with the pincer movement between thumb and first finger. He may have an unusually tight grip.

Social development
He is easily distracted in many situations. He may have poor eye contact, plays on his own and has a limited concentration span. He shows little

interest in the outside world; he does not point. Frustration causes him to have temper tantrums, and he becomes easily distressed.

Sensitivity
He is still sensitive to loud noises and intense light. Toilet training can be difficult, and the child can also have bowel problems.

Speech
He does not develop pre-speech sounds. During the first two years, be aware that children develop at vastly different rates, e.g. some children use only pre-speech sounds, while others use more recognisable words.

2–3 YEARS

Sleep
The child's difficulties with sleep continue, and sometimes he cannot sleep alone.

Eating
Feeding is still messy, and he has difficulty using a spoon and a fork. He is a picky eater.

Motor skills
He still has trouble with running, climbing, pedalling. Using a spoon and fork is difficult. He is very restless, and cannot stay in one place for long. He finds it hard to balance on one foot, and has difficulties placing his feet properly, e.g. he runs with an awkward gait, moves in a floppy manner, like an uncoordinated puppy. He has difficulty using handles on doors or co-ordinating pedals. He may exhibit repetitive head or finger movements. A dominant hand has not emerged.

Social development
As the child becomes aware of his difficulties, his frustration increases with frequent angry outbursts, sulking, or other difficult behaviour. He still needs attention and adult reassurance. The gap between normal accepted behaviour and that of the child widens and becomes more obvious. He has a poor concentration span.

Sensitivity
He is sensitive to loud noises and startles easily. He over reacts to stimuli. The child is distressed when he has his nails or hair cut.

Speech
His speech is slow to develop and even regresses.

3–5 YEARS

Sleep
He has an unsettled sleep pattern.

Eating
Feeding is still unsatisfactory. The child remains a messy and picky eater.

Motor skills
He is increasingly frustrated as his abilities are slow or fail to develop properly and lacks skills that other children have. He can still use either hand for tasks. He often swaps hands in mid task and does not use one hand consistently.

Gross motor skills
He moves awkwardly, trips, falls and has poor spatial awareness. He bumps into objects, has difficulty pedalling a tricycle or similar toy.

Fine motor skills
He cannot manipulate his fingers well. He might dislike puzzles and construction toys.

His grip of a pencil is either too tight or awkward.

He finds scissors difficult to manipulate.

His drawings of figures and objects are basic.

He has difficulty in dressing: buttons, zips and press-studs still frustrate him.

Social Development
The child is constantly fidgeting: he cannot sit still or get comfortable; his feet swing and tap; and his hands are on the move feeling or fiddling with some object or other.

He finds it hard to be part of a peer group because he does not know how to behave with them, he does not understand social situations, misses social signals and does not understand facial expressions or might have poor eye contact. His voice can become loud and shrill; he is easily excitable and easily distressed.

Peers find his behaviour bewildering, cannot make sense of it and become frustrated with him. They often shun the child. This is a cycle of misunderstanding, which alienates him further from his peers, and the social difficulties the child is having are due to his innate problems.

Sensitivity

He is sensitive to loud noises and startles easily.

He finds intense lights difficult to cope with.

He has sensitive skin and finds labels, collars and waistbands in clothes are hard to bear.

He is still distressed when having his hair and nails cut.

Speech

His patterns of speech develop more slowly than those of his peers.

He finds it hard to concentrate on a given task.

He has difficulty in comprehending the sequences of rhymes and stories.

He does not respond quickly to verbal instructions, and finds it hard to absorb more than one instruction at a time.

He does not readily retrieve from his memory relevant information for a given situation.

Some dyslexic or dyspraxic children are very articulate and can express themselves clearly. However, others find it hard to make themselves understood.

5–7 YEARS

Sleep

He still does not sleep through the night, and some children do not want to sleep alone. He can have bad dreams and an over-active mind. He is uncomfortable in his body and is unable to settle.

Eating
He continues to eat untidily and is wary of new foods. He still prefers food that is easy to eat, and he might need to drink a lot of liquid.

Motor skills
Gross motor skills
He still can be clumsy, bump into things and drop things when putting them on to surfaces. He finds riding a bicycle or tricycle difficult. Catching, throwing and kicking balls can be hard. It is not obvious that he prefers one hand, eye, ear and foot over the other. He finds it hard to sit still easily.

Fine motor skills
Handwriting is proving difficult, and he finds it hard to colour in pictures and draw objects. He dislikes puzzles and constructional toys. He still has difficulty with doing up zips, fastening buttons, tying shoelaces and with the order in which he puts on his clothes.

Coordination
His coordination between hand and eye is poor, and he has trouble with spatial awareness, together with inaccurate perceptions.

Social Development
Refer back to the signs and symptoms for the 3–5 years age group. However, some of the items become more significant. When immature behaviour persists, long after children of a similar age are coping in social situations, there is real cause for concern.

The child does not learn readily from experience and does not transfer skills from one situation to another.

He has difficulty understanding non-verbal communication, such as facial expressions, body language and being aware of other people's feelings or moods.

He finds it hard to make eye contact.

He still does not know the right order in which to put his clothes on and the order in which he should perform everyday tasks.

Sensitivity
Refer to ages 3–5 years.

Speech

He still has difficulties in pronouncing words correctly and getting them in to the right sequence. His development of linguistic skills might have been slow, even though he has an excellent vocabulary, he uses it in an unusual way.

He does not learn and recite rhymes as he should. He fails to distinguish similar words such as ball and call because of their similar pronunciation.

He has difficulty in discriminating between different sounds such as b|p|d, g|j, u|y, l|f, f|v|th.

He does not pay attention when spoken to, he shows no interest in listening to stories, and he fails to understand explanations.

Educational problems

His progress in reading, writing and spelling is poor, contrary to expectations built up by normal development in other respects. He finds it difficult to blend letters together into recognisable words. He might misread or omit word endings such as 'ing', 'ed', 'er', 's' and small words. The child sometimes adds extra words or changes words (surprisingly, the changes made by the child often make sense in context). He has difficulty breaking words into syllables and assembling them to make a word. He finds reading aloud very hard work and does not always understand what he has read. He cannot pick out the main points in a story.

Although the child appears bright in many ways, he might find it incomprehensible that words can be read in only one way. For example, he argues that whichever way one looks at a mug, it is still a mug. He does not understand that there is only one way to read the word 'mug' because the letters appear in his mind as 'mgu', 'umg', 'gum'. He might even see the letter 'M' as 'W', 'E' or '3' as the letters flip around for him.

He writes mirror images of letters and has difficulty in forming letters and writing them down in some reasonable state of order. He is constantly confused with b|d|p, g|j, u|y, m|n, s|z.

He does not know the times of the day or sequences of events. He might not be able to remember personal details such as the date of his birthday and his home address.

The child might find counting hard work, and so he uses sticks or fingers to help.

He finds it hard to deal with abstract concepts, but he usually copes better when the problem is explained using more 'concrete' materials such as sticks or cubes for mathematics.

He has tantrums as a result of frustration, or daydreaming caused by sensory overload. There is too much information to absorb easily, and so he simply switches off or erupts.

He develops work-avoidance tactics such as offering to do 'jobs', make trips to toilet, etc.

He is very easily distracted in the classroom and can develop poor behaviour, e.g. become the class clown.

He is often very tired as a result of the extra effort and concentration required in the classroom.

He might be reluctant to go to school after a positive start.

7–13 YEARS

Sleep
The child has trouble settling down to sleep, possibly because of excess adrenaline and an over-active mind, often reliving the frustrating experiences of the day, focusing on the negative and becoming distressed. He has difficulty in shutting off and relaxing. He might still fear being alone.

Eating
Meals can become a battlefield because the child still eats in an immature, even ill mannered way, e.g. general sloppiness, noisy and overfull mouth. The child should have learnt to eat in an acceptable manner by this age.

Motor skills
Gross motor skills
He still finds it difficult to catch and kick balls, and to carry out instructions in the gym, sports field, or dancing class.

He has severe confusion between left and right.

He has not mastered the skills needed to ride a bicycle.

He has difficulty balancing and standing on one foot, hopping, jumping and doing forward and backward rolls.

Fine motor skills

Poor pencil grip and difficulty with handwriting and colouring in pictures cause the child to tire.

Dressing can still be difficult because he cannot tie laces or fasten buttons or zips and still does not know in what order to put on his clothes.

Holding and manipulating his knife, fork and spoon are still problems.

Using scissors and other such tools can be difficult.

Social Development

First refer to ages 5 to 7.

The difficulties experienced by 5–7 year old children continue even though the child is older and more mature. The child finds it difficult to organise and easily forgets what is expected of him, e.g. what he needs for school, lessons, sport kit, etc.

He needs lots of attention and reassurance about everyday life, and he seems to become unduly concerned about minute details that would seem irrelevant to most children. At this stage children become more aware of their social inadequacies, and this increases their general frustration and lowers their self-esteem.

The child does not forget slights, which are common in tween-age behaviour.

Sensitivity

By this age children learn to cope with many sensitivities but can still react badly to light, noise and texture of material. However, one should remember that it is an added stress and might be the reason for outbursts and bad behaviour.

Speech

The child still does not communicate his ideas easily, put his ideas in the right order or select the correct information.

He cannot recall the specific words easily and is inclined to substitute more general words instead, e.g. 'whatyoumaycallit'

He can be obsessive about finishing his explanations whether they are relevant or not.

Some children appear to have difficulty in understanding what is said to them, and there is a time lag before they answer. They seem to have to translate each sentence into their own language before they can answer, and then translate that answer into ordinary English.

The child takes language literally and does not understand nuances.

Educational

The child's lack of progress in reading, writing and spelling are much more noticeable now and contrast with his development in other respects.

Sometimes blending sounds together can cause him to become confused. For instance, when deciphering a word such as 'together', he might break the word down into the sounds 'to', 'get', 'her'. He blends these sounds and says 'to-get-her'. He does not recognise the resulting word as 'together', so he becomes confused and cannot give any meaning to this new word.

When working on written material, he prefers to use familiar short words rather than try a new word and spell it incorrectly - these are usually written phonetically or by guesswork. He might fail to use link words such as 'and', 'of', 'on'.

He has little idea of punctuation when writing or reading.

His written stories are often brief, sometimes lack sequence, and often show weak development of the storyline or characters.

He might be able to tell a story verbally easily but finds it almost impossible to write it down.

When reading aloud or writing, he can confuse or transpose letters in the following groups, b|d|p, w|m, u|y, u|n, j|f, v|f|th. Letter combinations such as 'str' can cause him difficulties.

If he is still struggling with his reading, he may complain of feeling unwell while reading, say he cannot see the letters properly, or make up any excuse not to read. There may, in fact, be a visual perception problem causing letters or words to move, flip, and even merge together. There are specialist opticians who you can consult on these matters.

He might be keen to read but when he does so, he changes tenses, add plurals and words, but the text may still make sense.

He may find small words such as 'saw' and 'was' difficult to decipher, together with 'of', 'far', 'for' and 'far', 'for', and 'from'.

When the child copies work from the blackboard, lines are missed and letters and numbers are transposed. Some children also find the same difficulty when copying from a textbook because they constantly lose their place.

The child might still reverse digits, e.g. '24' for '42' when doing arithmetic, and is confused by the symbols such as '+' and '×' and the symbols for more than '>' and less than '<'.

He cannot remember multiplication tables, particularly their sequence, the order of the days of the week, months of the year, and the alphabet.

He is slow in learning to tell the time and can confuse concepts such as yesterday, today and tomorrow.

The child might have difficulties with music; he cannot keep time or understand musical notation. He is likely to prefer a string, brass or wind instrument to the piano.

His handwriting is still poor, with reversals and weak letter formation and inappropriate use of capital letters.

He has difficulty recalling words, especially when writing them down.

For the above reasons, the child's life can become increasingly stressful.

13–18 years

Sleep
The child might still tire easily. He finds it difficult to keep going all day, and might need one or more periods of complete rest during the day. Often he might need two or three days off school each term just to keep going.

Eating
He still eats messily or in an ill mannered way. By this age, it is likely that the child will have developed some tactics to mask this behaviour.

Motor control
Gross motor skills
The child can still be clumsy and find team games difficult. He might learn skills to play a team game well enough on his own, but struggle to apply these skills in a team situation. Anticipating the moves of other players might also cause difficulties. His balance might still be poor, so that he cannot change direction quickly in team sports.

These difficulties can diminish both his self-esteem and the esteem of his peers.

Fine motor skills
He still has difficulty with handwriting. By this age, he has usually developed and mastered the skills needed to dress himself.

Social development
The child can become isolated and lonely; this leads to feelings of frustration and low self-esteem.

Sensitivity
The teenager might still not tolerate bright lights, some cloth fabrics, noise, different tones and pitches, and music from another child's Walkman can irritate. A young child's screech or crying may cause the teenager to become irritable and bad tempered. Teenagers can have a greater sensitivity to failure than normal.

Speech
Some teenagers cannot express their ideas quickly or clearly. The inability to express themselves clearly is often made worse by the additional stress of being teenagers.

Educational
The teenager still makes frequent spelling mistakes. Copying from the blackboard can result in inaccuracies or losing the place and getting sentences muddled.

Planning essays can be a burden because he cannot sequence his ideas logically or develop arguments. His choice of words can be restricted because he cannot spell well or cannot readily recall the words he wants to use.

He has difficulty taking notes, either because he does not understand the main points or because of poor spelling. Taking notes from speech is especially difficult. He might be unable to make sense of his notes later, when they are needed for an essay, or for revision.

He might misunderstand questions in comprehension. Answering exam questions can prove difficult because of the processes involved and ways of interpreting the information.

Reading might remain slow, and so reading any text at secondary level places the child at a disadvantage.

Learning foreign languages often proves difficult, and French more so than others.

HELP

INTRODUCTION

This chapter is mainly for parents, but teachers and classroom assistants and carers could also find it helpful when dealing with these children and their parents. For parents, there is a great deal of information, but it will encourage them to feel more positive about the situations they face and have some constructive things to do to help their children.

THINK DIFFERENTLY

Always make the child feel very special and loved.

Stop looking at your child with a critical eye. See his special uniqueness and concentrate on his positive attributes. When he is successful, show delight and praise.

Give the child lots of positive attention. Emphasise what he can achieve and all the things he does well (no matter how small). Build esteem.

What is perfect? We all have something wrong with us, e.g. funny walk, wear glasses, braces on our teeth, big ears, skinny legs. So we must acknowledge that we are all different from one another.

Spend as much time as you can talking to the child. Be sure to listen to him and try and understand what he is saying.

Do not shout. This will only enhance the child's frustration, making him feel badly about himself. What he has done needs to be understood, and it is important to point out that it can be sorted out and put right.

Set clear and consistent boundaries. Be seen to be fair and firm when applying them. Having said that, there may be times when you are constantly battling. Then you might need to take time out and perhaps not 'take the bait' if you feel the child is simply looking for a reaction.

Try to ignore bad behaviour and praise good behaviour, but first explain to the child what you are going to do very clearly.

Give clear instructions for his age and ability.

Children with difficulties can be very demanding. However, they are often very loving and sensitive too. They require a lot of time and patience. Managing behaviour is a subtle art and needs a great deal of understanding, patience and intuition.

These children need a lot of structure in their lives, and they need to be encouraged to want to help themselves.

Finally accept that the child has a problem and do something about it. Accepting the fact that it is not the child's fault is important, and finding help as soon as possible will greatly ease the situation. Each child is his own person, and it is your job to help him fulfil his own potential.

Doing something is a positive step for carers, so you lose the feeling of helplessness. When you all realise that the child has a problem for which he can receive help you can all make positive progress.

Armed with the appropriate information and knowledge of what is available, you can begin to make informed choices.

There are no quick fixes. This is a life-long learning process for parents and children who need to think differently.

HELP FOR 0–5 YEARS

General health

If the child regularly has the volume of the television or radio very loud have his hearing checked. If he holds the book very close for reading, have his eyesight tested. He might have defective hearing or eyesight that is causing frustration and distress.

Check for allergies and intolerances to food such as milk, sugar, wheat and additives.

If a child is reluctant to catch a ball it might be because he does not perceive it correctly. His brain might not understand what his eyes see. He might also have difficulty co-ordinating his muscles.

Do not restrict the child to baby walkers or other devices that limit movement for a long time.

Speech

If the child's speech needs correcting do it gently and not too frequently. The child will want to talk about his difficulties and must be encouraged to get past the blame and frustration and move on to solving their problems. By doing this he will become happier and more confident.

If speech is late in development, e.g. poor word order, general immaturity of speech, lack of understanding of tenses and lots of mispronounced words, then speech therapy might be needed. Have the child's speech evaluated by the local speech therapist. This help can usually be obtained through your family doctor.

What you can do to help

In this section, we have listed some of the things that you can do as a parent.

- Encourage crawling because this is an important part of development.
- Encourage gross motor activity such as running, swimming, ball games, play in adventure playgrounds, etc.
- Encourage the child to do jigsaws, which will help him to understand the concepts of parts into a whole and how ideas develop.
- Encourage saying and repeating rhymes and jingles, singing songs and telling short stories, which have repetition in them such as 'The Three Little Pigs'. Rhyming, remembering and listening are all necessary for the development of literacy skills.
- Encourage the child to discover the world and talk about what he is seeing, putting the information into a familiar context.
- Encourage discussions about days of the week and what happens on each day, e.g. Monday swimming, Tuesday visit Granny, etc. Follow this by introducing the months of the year, birthdays, festivals, seasons, stressing all the time their places in the sequence of annual events.
- Encourage discussion about groups of animals, plants and everyday objects into appropriate categories, e.g. that table, chair, couch and desk are furniture.
- Encourage crafts such as painting, working with clay, cutting and sticking.
- Encourage stacking and building bricks, Lego, Connect and other play activities, which encourage fine motor control and co-ordination between hand and eye.
- Encourage recognition of right and left. Use songs to reinforce the idea, e.g. 'Hokey-cokey', '1, 2, 3, 4, 5 once I caught a fish alive'. Put shoes and trainers in the correct position, saying left and right as they put them on. Set the table, emphasising that the knife is on the right and the fork on the left.

- Encourage the child to see the sequence of putting his clothes on in the correct order.
- Encourage him to cope with buttons, zips, poppers, Velcro, ties and shoelaces. Choose clothes with the minimum of problems at first, but persist until all the necessary skills are learnt.
- Encourage the whole family to play matching and sequencing games together with board games. Show your delight when the child is successful or when he shows signs of improvement.
- Encourage eye movements from left to right. When you begin reading with your child move your finger under the words as you read. Find his name or a word he likes and let him read it.
- Encourage reading. Make it comfortable and enjoyable. Start with small books and read only while the child is happy to listen. Make it fun. Little and often usually works well and slowly builds up his attention span.
- Encourage the child to recognise his name when written with a capital letter and lower case letters, e.g. Ben. Put his name on his bedroom door and in other places so he will see it regularly and remember it.
- Encourage the learning of the sound and names of the letters in the alphabet and relate them to the symbols. Lower case letters should be taught first followed by the upper case, e.g. the sound 'a' (as in cat) should be matched with the symbols a and A.
- Encourage counting by grouping everyday objects in pairs and groups. Make a collection of similar things and those that are different. Count mugs, spoons, forks, etc. Introduce the collective words such as fruit and furniture.
- Encourage the child to know the names of things and the concepts of same and different and odd one out.
- Encourage the child to write numbers correctly, writing the number large on a white board or piece of paper. Then ask the child to trace it with the index finger of the hand he writes with. Repeat the process several times on different surfaces so that he will get the feel of it. Skywriting can also help. Associate numbers with their values.
- Encourage the child to recognise numbers in everyday life, such as house numbers, prices and speed limit signs.
- Encourage all physical activities such as dancing, karate, tai chi, judo, swimming, horse riding, etc. This will develop co-ordination, confidence and self-esteem.

• Encourage the child to learn his full name, address and telephone number.

HELP FOR 5–7 YEARS

When the child goes to school, he might be diagnosed as having special needs. If so, specialist teaching can be a great help. Hard work and co-operation can achieve success. However, the teaching should be a positive experience, and if it is not, try to find another 'teacher'.

Teaching should be fun and enjoyable and often with a safe routine so the child knows what to expect. However, gentle pressure to produce good work and more of it each time is also important. It should be structured so that the child achieves success at every stage. Further, it should be reinforced in an interesting way. Multi-sensory techniques should be used, and this means using the senses of hearing, sight and touch together with speech.

Cursive handwriting helps children with difficulties and aids their spelling. Look for special pencils and holders to make writing easier.

Phonics or sounds should be built into words quickly so that they have meaning. The words should then be put into sentences and written down. It is important to listen to the child and be flexible in your approach. Sometimes phonics do not work, and sight word methods (flash cards, etc.) work better, or a combination of both methods. We are all individuals and learn in our own ways.

Reading can be made more fun when the adult reads with the child. At first, the adult should read quietly at the same time as the child does. This enables him to hear the story and make sense of what he is reading. Then move on to reading alternate pages. Read to him missing out a word here and there, which he has to put in quickly. Then the child can do the same, so he does not lose face if he does not know the word. Read regularly in short bursts and stop when concentration is lost. However, show your delight when he reads more than expected. Keep the reading material at his level and gradually increase the complexity so he feels successful all the time. Let the child choose a book, magazine or comic so that he can experience pleasure and enjoyment through reading.

Work on the sequencing of numbers to help the child to learn the order by frequent repetition. Help him to listen to numbers such as 23, so that he writes 2 first followed by 3. The teen numbers are more difficult to grasp and can need a lot of work to understand and remember.

To overcome learning difficulties, one must first accept that there is a problem, and then develop strategies and means to cope in order to minimise the stress and maximise potential.

The child will have bad days when he seems unable to remember things that he has previously learnt. Fortunately, these times pass. Make light of these difficult days and focus on the successes of the good days.

It is important that the child with special needs or learning difficulties is encouraged to practise and develop his skills at all times. Without constant reinforcement he may lose his hard-gained achievements, and it will take further intensive effort to relearn. This should be done in a way that is fun.

When working, continue as long as you have the child's attention, enthusiasm and interest. When he loses interest, take a break, but plan the next part of the session by setting goals, challenging and sparking his curiosity.

The child might need to relax at first and then do his homework. He is likely to get very tired as he is working so much harder than his peers.

HELP FOR 7–13 YEARS

If at the age of seven plus, the child is still having problems with reading, writing, spelling or mathematics, but seems bright in other ways, and is developing and growing normally, he needs help.

Have his hearing and eyesight checked and, if all is well, go to the school and discuss the problems with the head teacher.

The School Psychological Service could help. At this stage accept the help offered. It should be on a one-to-one basis, carefully structured and multi-sensory (using the senses of sight, hearing, touch and speaking). Watch the child's progress closely. If you are not satisfied, seek a second opinion.

Encourage the child to develop interests of his own, e.g. swimming, art, making a collection, so that he feels he is succeeding. This will boost his self-confidence.

A child of this age group needs much attention; read to him, talk to him, listen to him and work with him. If you give him this attention, it will help him to come to terms with his difficulties and accept them. He will then be encouraged to work hard and to overcome his special difficulties.

Help him to organise his life by making a timetable, writing down things he needs, e.g. Monday – violin, Tuesday – P. E. clothes, etc. Be firm that *he* does the remembering and makes the preparations for the day.

The concentration span of the child is often limited, so it is important to gauge how long he can work easily. End the task before he loses concentration, so preventing further frustration.

Remember that he tires easily and might need time doing little in order to recover.

Some children have to concentrate hard while watching television. This might be because, if they do not, they lose the thread of the story completely and it means nothing to them.

Encourage reading by letting the child read easy books and comics to start with. Help him to develop this skill by introducing books with a small amount of print, gradually increasing this as he succeeds. Let him read the books he wants to read, and do not force him to read the ones you wish him to read.

Read aloud to the child every day. Introduce books that he should be reading but is failing to read. Encourage him to watch the text and get him to put in words that you miss out while continuing to read. This helps him to move his eyes. Then suggest that he reads a short passage at regular intervals. It can help to use a piece of card to isolate the line being read, or point to the words with a pencil or finger. At suitable intervals, go back over the events of the story to help him to remember the sequence of the story line, the characters involved, to make sense of the text and to absorb and retain what he has heard.

Make sure that he knows the days of the week and months of the year and help him with the alphabet. Show him how to use simple dictionaries and reference books.

Check that he can tell the time using analogue and digital clocks. If not, help him beginning with the hours and half hours. Develop his understanding into the 24-hour clock and its use in bus and train timetables.

Continue teaching multiplication tables. If this proves to be difficult, teach the accurate use of a table card. It could help to explain the situation to the school. Persist in trying to get him to learn the tables. They are valuable in many situations in daily life.

Use squared paper when dealing with decimals. If the decimal point is in a square of its own then accurate addition, subtraction should follow.

Continue to play ball games, board games and card games with him.

Check for confusion between left and right. Help the child by developing some compensating aid, e.g. writing with the right hand, wearing his watch on the left.

Choosing a secondary school is important. If the child is still not coping and no help seems available, then you should discuss the matter with the new Head Teacher, Year Tutor or Counsellor to find out what can be done.

As a parent, you almost certainly know your child better than his teacher. Nevertheless, teachers have experience of many more children than you have and have much to offer. Bear in mind that they are also human and can have difficulties in understanding a new situation about which they may know very little. In trying to obtain help from school, be understanding and polite as well as firm and persistent.

HELP FOR 13–18 YEARS

At this age, children are more aware of their problems, and can understand the implications of the problems. So discuss with your child whether he still feels the need for some specialist help. If he agrees, go ahead and find the appropriate help. If he is unwilling, be patient – it is likely that the child will recognise the need and accept your suggestions.

Encourage your child to learn to type accurately and to use computers and word processors. This will mean that he can produce beautiful pieces of work that look attractive.

Small hand-held tape recorders can be useful to record lessons (with the teachers' permission) and when revising. Some people learn better through listening than through written work.

Electronic notepads or laptop computers can be used for recording details of homework and other messages about school life, e.g. details of after-school activities, games or music lessons. 'Post it' notes can remind children of things that need their attention.

Teach mind mapping where links between concepts, rather than the sequencing of events is a priority. This helps with both essays and revision.

Good study skills help with revision, and making notes and exam techniques are essential for all pupils.

Discuss with the school teachers the choice and number of subjects to be taken in exams. Important factors in this choice are the child's interest, success already achieved in the subjects and his hopes for the future. To take fewer subjects and succeed could be preferable to taking too many, which might lead to excess pressure, failure and despondency.

Still encourage success in activities out of school, e.g. football, chess, games, stamp collecting. It is helpful if these activities include mixing with other people, as some children can find social interaction difficult.

As your child approaches his final two years at school and school leaving examinations, contact the school and ask for details of the examining boards the school will be using. The use of an amanuensis (hand writer) and or a computer is allowed in special circumstances. Additional help can also be given in national tests. Telephone or write to the examining board for the school to discover the allowances it makes for pupils with special needs and how the allowances can be arranged. Discuss the pros and cons of having extra time with your children and abide by your child's wishes. To take advantage of the allowances, a report from an Educational Psychologist might be needed, and the report must be obtained by a deadline.

At a later date, when your child is applying for jobs, colleges or universities, discover as much as is possible about the jobs or courses so that he will have the maximum chance of fulfilling his potential.

When you and your child are considering future careers for him, look into as many ways of obtaining the chosen goal as you can. It helps to choose non-academic courses. It might take longer to achieve the goal, but the steps would be easier. A course that includes practical work and a written project, which can be done at the candidate's own pace and counts towards the exam, could be helpful.

Children with special needs often seem to mature later than their friends, so they will need more attention, and encouragement, even persuasion to keep them going.

These can be hard times for parents. So often, all that parents can do is to stand back and watch. Young people can be stubborn. If they do not want help then it will not benefit them at all. Forcing help upon them will probably just cause further distress to all concerned. However, parents should continue to celebrate their child's successes and commiserate with their child's failures.

CONCLUSION

In this book, we have set out what we believe from our own experience to be important signs and symptoms in children who are not fulfilling their potential and are often worried by their lack of success.

Each child is a special individual, and if he has serious difficulties in learning then he will need understanding, support, and often specialist treatment to help him to become happier, more confident and be able to fulfil his potential.

We hope that when you have read this book you will be able to think in a more informed way, become more flexible in your approaches, and move confidently forward.

PERSONAL STORIES

JW's STORY

Where to begin? It was my first pregnancy and a very exciting time. In the last trimester I can remember feeling very uncomfortable. Boy, could this baby move around! It almost felt like he could wrap his fingers around my ribs!! The day finally came when we had had enough waiting and the doctors were convinced it was time, but I needed a little help. JW was induced. It had been 17 hours, and the baby was in distress. I now needed serious help and it was off for an emergency caesarean. It was a bit touch and go with husband reporting the baby was very blue with a 3 apgar score, but he soon recovered.

Even before we left hospital JW was extremely demanding. This baby wanted to feed all the time. I can remember the nurses saying this boy just will not give you a chance. A few weeks later a visiting midwife made a funny comment about the baby not being settled and wished me luck. It was just one of those comments and the way she said it, that made me wonder. But this is my beautiful first baby. We seemed to reach all the milestones, if not in time, a bit early. This wonderful boy seemed to skip stages and even progressed quickly to walking without crawling. JW liked constant movement. He took his first steps between 9 and 10 months and was the only baby out of my NCT group who was walking 'well' at the first birthday party of the group. What a clever boy. I can remember lots of falls and lots of big bumps on his head. Maybe it wasn't such a good thing to start walking so young. And another thing, we had loads of ear infections, which were treated with antibiotics.

As I was pregnant with number two I thought it would be a good idea to get JW involved in a nursery program a few days a week. I did not want the new baby to arrive and have JW feeling he was being pushed away. I wanted to establish a good routine before number two brought along complications. So, we started in a gentle nursery, run from a woman's home 2-3 mornings a week. All seemed to be going well except...one evening my husband ran into a colleague and found his child was in the same nursery...oh the stories he heard about this one terribly behaved child. Funny we hadn't heard about him. Oh yes, that JW!!

If I only knew then, what I know now.

Kindergarten. Nothing that raised a red flag, though he often was not part of the group and would wander around the room preferring his own company. JW did not have many friends, and we were busy with baby brother so, nothing was really wrong but something just wasn't right.

Junior school. JW's birthday is in June, so he is young for his year. He had difficulty sitting still, was easily distracted, still wet at night, and had few friends. We began to notice strange attachments – I wasn't allowed to throw anything out, e.g. broken kettle. JW recalls first instances of feeling picked on. He didn't quite fit in. We began to notice strange and inappropriate behaviours.

We moved to new school and...lots of little problems. Yes, I am sure I was an anxious mother but something just wasn't right.

Academically JW was getting on well enough. However, we had concerns about his spelling, handwriting and, yes, his social behaviour. Behaviours that are a bit different become a bit awkward when a child gets older and peers do begin to notice. JW would come home and say he felt like a bit of old rag thrown down in the street. No one would play with him and worse...he was being teased, made fun of and excluded. This was very difficult to deal with, along with coming to terms with being a part of the problem.

Luckily, it was at this point that we met Jean and for the first time someone said yes there is something wrong and I think I know what you should look into doing. And this was the start of our journey. We began with brush stroking. We only now understand that we were quite a complicated case and, yes, we had great success. JW was much more together, much better coordinated. However, we still had much anger, frustration and countless other issues to deal with. We moved on to homeopathy, which has been very helpful and supportive for the whole family. Once again we have seen improvement, but...we had a long way to go.

At about this point I finally began to understand that we had a real puzzle here. We didn't have a firm diagnosis because we didn't fit neatly into any category. We had difficulties similar to those that have dyslexia, dyspraxia, autistic spectrum difficulties, and ADD. It became clear to me that no one treatment was going to fix or help our boy. I began to look at the different issues and look for people who could help each symptom. At this point I took a big step, against everyone's advice, and contacted LEAP (London's Early Autism Project). I decided we had to deal with the experts on social behaviour. This therapy opened doors and helped us to understand that JW just didn't get it. He often simply didn't understand social cues, interactions, and even facial expressions. This was one of the causes of major frustration for our boy. We could now address things in a different way…another great success…our focus changed from getting the world to understand JW to getting JW to understand the world. This was a major turning point.

Another piece of the puzzle fitted into place, and it became clear we had to look at something further. I heard about the Sunflower Method, which works on three levels: structural, mental and biochemical. Not only were the specialists able to improve further JW's coordination (we walked out of the office after the first visit and JW said 'my legs aren't floppy anymore' he had been putting so much energy into simply keeping himself upright), they were able to look at his biochemistry and supplement his deficiencies and check for allergies. We saw a sudden improvement of mood because he could really apply all of the things he had learned with LEAP. And on the mental level, JW often feels quite stressed. The Sunflower Method is helping him deal with everyday stresses. We are still working with the Sunflower Method and have found we have made lots of progress.

But there is still more…I finally realise we are part of the progress. Because of our second son's dyslexia we looked into the Davis Dyslexia method. I became interested in the concept that helped make links in sequencing, time, cause and effect and consequence and decided to jump in and have a go with JW. Once again we have moved up another level and are able to address things, which would never have been understood before.

We have tried to give JW as many tools and opportunities to help him to cope in this world. We were lucky because we definitely have benefited from all the different approaches we have used. I couldn't say which one was the best because they have all contributed their bit in putting the pieces together.

Through it all, our boy has had incredible courage. Yes, he has his highs and lows, but he has worked very hard to achieve where he is today. We have learned so much from him. He has faced struggles daily, with not understanding the world around him, not being able to control his body, not being able to control his perception, being the odd one out, being bullied, made fun of, teased. And yet, he gets up everyday and soldiers on.

HELEN'S STORY

Hi, my name is Helen; I am 33 and I have known that I am dyslexic since I was 18. I was diagnosed quite late in life. I struggled through school and was seen as below average, which suited me, as this meant no one had high expectations of me.

I do see benefits to being diagnosed dyslexic, it makes me determined to try task dyslexics find difficult. As a dyslexic, my motto is:

'I don't see it as what I can't do – I see it as what I can do differently.'

I had a number of hitches before I got to where I am now. When I left school I was determined to pursue a career in nursing. In order to take this route I had to gain an O level in English, no easy task for someone who has not been diagnosed as dyslexic. I had two attempts both of which I failed. When I sat this for the third time it was decided to send me to an educational psychologist. This was an experience in itself – I could never understand why this psychologist asked me to do numerous tasks, which I was destined to fail – leaving me feeling totally demoralised.

These tests were carried out over several sessions with the outcome being that I had a specific learning difficulty – this always confused me as if it was a specific difficulty. Why couldn't they be specific and tell me what it was? Once this was completed it was agreed I could have my exams read and written for me – not to mention that I went to an English class at school, went to an English night school and had a English tutor, so thankfully third time round I gained a C in my English O level and another four O levels into the bargain.

I was now in the position to start nursing. Life looked perfect for five months and then things went positively pear shaped, I was called to the nurse tutor who told me that due to my dyslexia I would never be able to complete my nurse training, that I would more than likely fail my finals and waste three years of my life. This was the end of my nursing training!

I can now see this as a positive turning point in my life, as I don't think I would have enjoyed nursing as a long-term career. I now work for a voluntary organisation developing and designing presentations, which people say are really pleasing on the eye, this I think is because I look at the shape of the words instead of reading them.

I don't think people are aware of how much dyslexia affects your day-to-day life. The world is designed for people who understand the written word. Allowances are made for hard of hearing, etc., in banks, building societies. Do you think there will ever be signs saying:

'Dyslexic Friendly – if you need help just ask'?

I think I cope well with my dyslexia and try to use my strengths to compensate for my weaknesses. It is very important to know your weaknesses, although it is possible to build on these. I have many coping mechanisms, as follows.

I am also totally honest with people about my dyslexia, so that they understand if I take longer to do something.

I take information home to read along with forms where I have time to read them and make sure I put the right information in the right place.

I keep a book of things I need to do at work.

I never use phone books, I use directory enquires on-line.

I don't leave people written messages – I e-mail all my messages.

The most important thing is I know my strengths and weaknesses – although I sometimes test myself to the limits to stretch myself, as the most important thing about dyslexics is that they are not stupid and their brain does get bored!

I do everything by computer – type letters, send e-mails, create my own cards – I can even type the inside of the cards to avoid having to write them over and over until they are right. The spell check is a god-send, although it does occasionally let me down. At work I had to confirm a venue with delegates for a training event, I confirmed it as West of Scotland Society for the *Dead*, it should have read *Deaf* – it did cause amusement.

Computers don't help with some day-to-day memory problems – some time ago I was out with a friend, as we passed her house she asked if I could run in and pick her up three things – a hairbrush, hairspray and her purse. I proudly came out with a toilet roll and a purse, when asked why I brought the toilet roll my reply was *'You have a cold'* – all you need is good understanding friends!

Finally I am proud to be dyslexic and think it is a quality – the world needs dyslexics who process information differently. Although if you are not dyslexic please don't be inclined to say you've got a touch of dyslexia today – I've heard this many times. Would people dream of saying I am a touch blind today???

MARK ON DYSLEXIA

I look back on my life, which is now some 37 years on. Dyslexia has affected me and other people in my life. I now have a good job working in London as a financial controller for a Design Co. in London. I am very happy and work with some great people. I have realised that I am an intelligent person and Dyslexia is a pain in the arse but it can be managed. With lots of effort it can be not much of a problem, but it will never go away.

Growing up was very confusing and stressful. I remember that between the ages of 5 and 11 I was incredibly bad at English and good at mental arithmetic. In those days, dyslexia was not as widely known as it is today. I was diagnosed when I was 9 years old. This upset both my parents greatly as they came from good academic families. At about this time I can remember writing a short story. I was sent to the headmaster who helped turn the story from $1\frac{1}{2}$ pages to 3 pages. Apparently I had missed out so many words. I did not understand. I was more interested in playing football, which I loved, and riding my bike.

I left junior school not being able to read a children's paperback. I had learnt to spell a few words. Secondary school was when dyslexia really kicked in. It hurt. I was lost in the big school with no real confidence in written work or any confidence to back it. The first year was very painful. I was lucky to be looked after by a couple of teachers. I was also able to play football, which gave me confidence.

The secondary years passed me by. In the seventies there was no great academic pressure. The only bright part was when I came top of the year in Economics, in the fourth year. This was a surprise to everyone because I was bottom of the class in everything else. Unfortunately, the teacher changed and that door closed. I left secondary school with a few qualifications and with a great deal of frustration. I felt academically useless and yet knowing that deep down I was bright and intelligent with no way of showing it.

Two incidents made me realise that I wanted to prove myself. One was a massive road accident, where I stopped breathing. Also, visiting one of my best friends parties at University and thinking this was great fun. These incidents got me moving. I embarked on a correspondence course doing Economic O and A levels. I passed to my great relief, receiving grade B in both papers.

This allowed me to do a HND Business and Finance Course, which I passed with a distinction of which I am very proud. I was lucky to meet some great friends and have some good experiences. The college was very demanding. I avoided subjects that needed lots of writing. I did all the accountancy options because you do not have to write long essays or reports.

I left college with my qualification without believing in myself, or the qualification that I had worked so hard for. I had a couple of jobs in the next year, which I did not enjoy or find very rewarding.

I was very lucky when one of my best friends started his own company and asked me to join as an accountant-cum-office manager. We started with five people and now have grown to over 35 people. I am now the financial controller for one of the leading Design Companies in London. It has been very challenging and rewarding, and finally in spite of the handicap of dyslexia I have a great job working with lots of good people and I have a reasonable income, my own flat and car.

Dyslexia causes a great deal of anguish, upset, loss of confidence, fear, feeling useless, thick and incredibly stupid. It can make you feel vulnerable and lost in the world, which can be extremely unforgiving.

However, dyslexia makes you learn survival skills. You are always guarding yourself from mistakes and looking stupid. It makes you learn to anticipate situations or avoid difficulties. This gives you the ability to read and understand situations very quickly. Unfortunately, this is not a great way to live your life if you use it to protect yourself from doing things and taking sensible risks. If you do, you're going to miss out on so much, because life is to be lived and not to hide away from, just because you are dyslexic. It is giving away too much importance.

I would encourage all dyslexics to believe in themselves and the people around them to do the same. Dyslexia cannot be cured, but it can be contained with lots of hard work and determination. Willingness to learn and not be afraid to ask for help, because there are a staggering number of people who want to help.

Just ask and live life to the full.

MARY'S STORY

My name is Mary and I was born in July of 1952. I am the seventh child in a family of eight. We lived in a small village in the Bedfordshire area. We all attended the village school, which was an infant and junior school.

School was absolutely horrible for me (it's supposed to be the best years of your life), but I didn't enjoy it, unlike my brothers and sisters. I was hopeless at everything; I was an underachiever. I couldn't do P.E. or games; whenever there were teams to be chosen it was me who stood on the side until the last and a teacher had to say, 'Right Mary you go on that team', and everybody moaned, 'Does she have to Miss, she can't even catch a ball'. I was the clumsiest member of my family, I bumped into door handles, the sides of tables, I couldn't get through the largest gap.

Reading and writing was quite difficult for me, I had great trouble with my 'B's and 'D's, 'E's and 'C's and 'M's and 'W's. Sometimes I got them all mixed up and back to front. I found that I was okay at answering questions in class but when it came to exams and writing I didn't seem to be able to retain the information. When I was reading anything, I had to read it more than once, it just didn't make sense otherwise. Teachers and pupils alike used to bully me. I was always miserable at school, everything was just so hard.

I remember about the age of thirteen or fourteen instead of learning about Maths and Arithmetic I was given a catalogue and told to go and sit in the corner and cut pictures out and stick them in a scrapbook.

As I was an underachiever and was always told that I was lazy, didn't try hard, day-dreamed all the time, I just used to do whatever I was told, I didn't make an effort, never asked questions, just thought 'I am thick, I am stupid.' The system had given up on me.

It was decided that they would keep me on an extra year so that I could learn touch-typing, which is a skill that I took to quite well.

I was able to hold down my first two jobs, one as a ledger clerk and the other working in a garage.

I married at the age of eighteen and had two girls by the time I was 21 and divorced at 28.

I managed to read to my children when they were young, changing words when I needed to do so and they didn't seem to mind.

While the children were growing up I did all sorts of jobs including bar work, shop work and cleaning. It was whilst I was working in the local supermarket that I met my second husband and married him at the age of 32.

In the supermarket I worked in the butcher's department, and I worked with a lazy butcher and all of a sudden a light came on in my head. I suddenly realised that everything in life was know-how and if you had that need to know, and someone was willing to share their knowledge and teach you, then there wasn't anything you couldn't achieve. This is how I became a very good butcher, preparing and presenting meat like an expert. It was quite an art form.

However, at this time my husband encouraged me to develop my typing skills.

I started at the local college and it was here that for the first time ever in my life I actually passed an exam. I got an RSA qualification in typing, I also started to learn to drive, my confidence was beginning to grow. All of a sudden from being an underachiever and never achieving anything, I started doing things and going places.

I left the butcher's department and went to work at British Aerospace first as a waitress, and then after about a year and a half I went to work in the offices. This was the first interview that I have ever had where the manager who was interviewing me said, 'I have no doubt you can do the job, it's yours if you want it'. It was here that I took a fellow colleague into my confidence because I had to do a lot of writing and with his help I was able to cope successfully with my job. At times I pretended I needed my glasses to help me 'read' certain documents. You start learning to be crafty.

It was sitting around the conference tables at Aerospace dealing with these important men that I began to think I wasn't stupid after all.

It was at this time I heard about dyslexia and wondered if it might be me.

Redundancy at Aerospace led me to the Job Centre and on to training programmes and gave me the time to look into dyslexia.

Through the Hertfordshire Dyslexia Association I was assessed and found to have some difficulties and, yes, I was dyslexic and not thick!

With one to one support and extra classes at college I achieved what I thought was impossible.

I started doing a City and Guilds course with Wordpower which was all to do with communication skills, using all these sources and you had to put it together in an evidence based folder. I had to get these units that had different elements in them and they would cross match. I have achieved Wordpower stage 1 and 2, which was City and Guilds, A.E.B.s, which are adult educational boards 2 and 3, I even did an OCR in English Language.

When I joined the Revenue in 1991, I had just found out that I was Dyslexic and I was wearing it like a badge, I was excited. There was a reason for these difficulties – yes, I wasn't stupid anymore – there was something wrong with me. I wasn't just thick – I had a problem. The only thing to do with it was to deal with it.

I have managed through the Revenue to do an NVQ in Business Admin, Level 2, I'm also the office's First Aid Officer – I've done a first aid course and I'm about to retrain to do another one, I'm the Colleague Support Officer, Communications Officer and the Equal Opportunity Officer.

So dyslexics, don't give up – keep on believing in yourself and you never know where it may lead you.

TAKING IT FURTHER

INTRODUCTION

We have taken a very flexible approach to offering a variety of help and information. Each discipline can be of help to some children but not necessarily everyone, but still probably worth investigating. Our goal is to present a variety of choices.

There are no quick fixes and whatever method is chosen it will take dedication, determination and effort. Sometimes there are no immediate results, but these may appear later.

This section of the book is for information only. We neither recommend nor promote any particular treatment.

Each individual contributor neither recommends nor endorses another's contribution.

ANN BRERETON

Ann Brereton is a trained teacher and the mother of a graduate son who has dyslexia. She is a former vice-chair of British Dyslexia Association and initiated and taught the first B.D.A. 'Befriender' courses. Ann has been a school governor with responsibility for S.E.N., and after many years as Befriender and Committee member of Hertford-shire Dyslexia Association and is now a vice president of the H.D.A. She has kindly contributed the D.I.Y. Therapies and How to get Help from Schools.

D.I.Y. Therapies

There are many therapies on offer, but most are costly or have long waiting lists if they are free. The following activities can be done at home, for little or no cost. Remember, to be effective, all therapies should be <u>frequent</u>, (daily, if possible).

Activities are shown in **bold**, why they are useful in *italics*. Handy hints, and a breakdown of the activity into manageable parts, follow.

Ball catching for *motor skills, hand/eye co-ordination*
- hands together, close against the chest, forming a bowl
- adult throws ball into the bowl, child watching ball all the time
- child clasps the ball tightly, without moving hands away from body
- use 'patter' e.g. 'Hold tight!' (don't say, 'Catch!' – hands will shoot forwards, and ball will fall between arms!)

Jigsaws for *visual discrimination, step-by-step methods*
- sort all <u>edge</u> pieces from the rest. Say, 'What is an edge?'
- find the four corners, 'Two straight edges making a point'
- feel the edges, feel the points
- set out four corners on the table, then build the frame
- draw attention to colours/objects on the box lid
- start with six pieces; use a 'patter' e.g. 'knobs and holes' for shapes.

Skipping for *co-ordination, sequencing*
- check rope is correct length (hold rope in front, step on it; hands should be at waist height)
- start with rope touching ground behind heels
- flip rope over head (both hands working together)
- jump with <u>two feet together</u> over the rope, <u>feet together</u>, saying, 'Jump!'
- repeat, getting quicker, with child saying the 'patter', e.g. 'Over, JUMP! Over, JUMP!'
- feet together jumps may need to be practised separately.

Line Dancing for *sequencing, co-ordination*
- adult should 'model' steps in front
- may need a helper behind to whisper the 'patter'
- 'right and left' may be difficult; use 'window/door/wall' instead
- learn small movements first.

Percussion Instruments for *co-ordination, rhythm, self-control and spelling!*
- use drums, triangles, and tambourines
- many older children still cannot copy or sustain a rhythm

• if you cannot hear the <u>beat</u> you cannot hear the syllables in a word.
• show how to hold the instrument and the beater
• demonstrate the rhythm, <u>say</u> the rhythm
• ('ONE, two, three! ONE, two, three!')
• child copies, remembering to SAY the 'patter'
• adult may need to put hand gently over child's hand to give a smooth movement
• you may need to learn the 'patter' first, using walking or marching in time to the beat.

Friends for tea for *social skills*
• encourages sharing, waiting, turn taking
• invite <u>one</u> child at a time
• organise the time, don't leave them unsupervised
• making cakes, sandwiches for tea/picnic always goes down well
• water pistol fights in the garden are fun, but will need dry clothes!
• outings to cinema, ten-pin bowling, water fun help to make a child popular
• (invite the other parent as well as a safety precaution)
• Steer clear of <u>board games</u> with friends; disputes and disappointments are inevitable.

Horse riding for *co-ordination, confidence, respect for animals*
• this improves posture, limits tantrums, encourages a sense of responsibility, and allows expression of affection towards the horse
• always wear correct clothing, especially a hard hat
• use a recognised class, with a trained instructor
• tell instructor of child's difficulties and needs

Swimming for *co-ordination, confidence, life skill, sequencing*
• water confidence is a life-saving skill
• most swimming clubs have a beginners class; can you (or a helper) be in the pool?
• explain your child's difficulties to the instructor
• swimming pools have lots of echoes; child should be at <u>front</u> of group when instructions are given
• child <u>must</u> look at instructor (lip-read!) when instructions are given
• trainer should ask child to 'repeat back' to check for understanding

Dressing for *life skill, sequencing*
- this is called <u>Reverse Chaining</u>
- parent lays out clothes <u>in correct order</u> on bed L to R
- <u>parent</u> dresses child (starting on the L) UNTIL last item (?jumper)
- <u>child</u> puts on jumper (parent praises, 'Look, you're dressed!')
- child stands in front of long mirror, parent recites the clothes <u>in correct order</u> (even the 'hidden' items)
- the next week, child puts on last two items

It may take some considerable time before the child will cope with <u>all the clothes</u>, even when the parent is laying them out in order. But the sooner you start, the sooner the child will be saved embarrassment at school. It is recognised that many children become school refusers on P.E. days because they cannot dress themselves.

Paying attention – 1 for *learning, social skills*
If you can't pay attention, you can't learn. And friends like it when you give them attention.
- the whole family must help
- agree that at suppertime, <u>everyone</u> must look at the person talking
- if the child's attention wanders, the speaker must <u>stop talking in mid-sentence</u>
- once a child's attention is re-focused, speaker continues
- don't forget to praise, 'I like the way you looked at Lucy whilst she was speaking.'

Paying attention - 2 for *learning, reading*
- when reading to child, encourage child to watch <u>your</u> finger move below the text
- if possible, get the <u>child</u> to follow text with own finger
- if concentration falters (e.g. child looks away from book) then <u>stop reading</u> in mid-sentence. No need to say anything, just wait quietly until attention is re-focused.

Blowing for *speech*
Here are two ways to blow a tissue from your hand:
- 'Big O' (wide open mouth, saying "h - ugh!")
- 'Little O' (pursed lips, ready to say "p - ugh! b - ugh!"

Blowing out <u>candles</u> with 'Big and Little O' is great fun! But remember to have a safe environment.

Remember, don't start a programme unless you can continue it on a regular basis. And use a repetitive 'patter' if necessary.

Copyright Ann Brereton

How to get help from schools

Having a child with Special Educational Needs (**S.E.N.**) usually means parents have two major worries: 'Is my child happy at school?' and 'Is my child receiving <u>appropriate</u> help, <u>sufficient</u> help to ensure good progress?' To answer these questions (which need to be asked throughout the school years) try and form a good relationship with the **Class Teacher**, **Form Tutor** or **Year Head**. Always book appointments, and go prepared with a written checklist. Do not get angry! Use phrases such as, 'I hear what you are saying **but**…' to press the point. All Local Education Authority (**L.E.A.**) schools must have regard to the **SEN Code of Practice**, which is available FREE from DFES publications on: 0845-60-222-60. Also ask for the **Toolkit**, which is an easy read and full of good suggestions. Take a Befriender (from a voluntary organisation) or a Parent Supporter (from the L.E.A.) to meetings.

The Code says that <u>all</u> teachers are teachers of SEN pupils, and that the curriculum must be **differentiated** i.e. different groups, work sheets, and homework. At the first meeting, ask how the school is helping your child. What are the school's concerns? If appropriate, ask for a copy of the child's current Reading Age (R.A.), Arithmetic Age (A.A.) and Spelling Age (S.A.). This is called the **Baseline Assessment**, and at your next meeting (which should be within a term) you can ask for updates on the R.A., S.A. and A.A. You may also need to discuss Language Skills, Co-ordination, Social Skills and Behaviour, etc.

If you are not happy, ask for a **Record** of the difficulties and a **Folio** of work, reports, etc., to be started. The Code calls this **School Action** and part of this will be an **Individual Ed. Plan** (**I.E.P.**). This will list **Targets**, **Programmes**, (who will do what and when), and set a **Review** date. You <u>and your child</u>, even young children) will be consulted about the I.E.P. It is an important document so make sure you have a dated copy.

School Action means that your child receives extra help, not just differentiated curriculum. '**Adequate Progress**' (Code Para 6.49) at meeting targets should be made. Parents should think about arranging medical appointments with Speech and Language Therapists, Physiotherapists, etc.

Failure to make 'adequate progress' is a signal for the help to move to **School Action Plus**, where outside **Experts** are brought in. These can be Advisors, Teachers, Educational Psychologists, School Medical Officers, etc. Parents should give copies of any medical reports for the Folio to the **S.E.N. Coordinator** (SENCO). Your child will still have an **I.E.P.**, but the outside experts will probably monitor progress. Some L.E.A.s will also allocate extra money to the school at this point, but some schemes are not ring-fenced for a particular child; schools are allowed to pool the extra S.E.N. money to provide, for example, smaller classes. This benefits <u>all</u> the children and therefore may not give sufficient help to the S.E.N. child.

If you are still unhappy with the <u>amount</u> and <u>type</u> of help given to your child, the next step is to write and ask the L.E.A. for a **Statutory Assessment** leading to a **Statement** of S.E.N. A child who has a **Statement** from the L.E.A. has a legal guarantee that these Needs will be met (providing the Needs are properly set out, and with the Provision detailed and specific). Statementing takes approximately 6 months of Statutory Assessment reports from school, Educational Psychologist, Medical Officer and (sometimes) Social Services, together with the view of parents and child. It is a good idea to submit as many <u>additional</u> reports as possible so that a full picture of your child's difficulties is seen.

For example:

- Any other **MEDICAL** reports
- Pediatrician
- Occupational Therapist
- Speech and Language Therapist
- Physiotherapist
- Psychiatrist
- G.P.
- Dietician
- Optician
- Audiologist.

Independent Educational Psychologist's report
Check the fee before making the appointment (approximately £300-£600)

Independent Tutor report

Photocopy all reports three times; one to send to the L.E.A., one for you to scribble on, and one 'clean' copy for your file. Keep a neat **file** of all letters, reports in date order. Also keep a **diary** of meetings (what was said and agreed), telephone calls, and when documents and letters are received.

Even if the L.E.A. agrees to a Statutory Assessment there is no guarantee that a Statement will be written. Although an Appeal can be made to an S.E.N. Tribunal, only children with the most severe educational needs will be Statemented, based on criteria in the Code, and evidence from the school that extra help so far has not led to 'adequate progress'. If a **draft Statement** is issued, refuse to accept Provision that is described as 'regular' or 'as necessary'. Provision must be detailed and specific.

Of course, there are parts of the national core curriculum, which will help a pupil with learning difficulties. For example, the **National Literacy Strategy** is phonically (sound) based and some spelling rules are taught. The **National Numeracy Strategy** provides opportunities for over-learning, but <u>mental</u> arithmetic is a strong element. There are also 'catch up' programmes in Year 2 and Years 7/8, but not all children with S.E.N. will qualify. The National programmes are 'pacey' and may be too fast for some S.E.N. children; a good I.E.P. or Statement can make these a meaningful time.

If you are dissatisfied with the school provision, always talk to the S.E.N.C.O. or Head Teacher. There is also a Governors' **S.E.N. Appeal Panel**, which can be useful if money (or 'resources') becomes an issue (schools have an amount in their general budget to spend on S.E.N., plus extra money to spend for Statemented pupils and perhaps on School Action Plus).

Finally, remember that you cannot have what is not there! If there is no L.E.A. provision in your area for, say, dyslexia or speech and language, why not join with other parents to lobby both Councillors (who allocate money) and L.E.A. Officers (who plan the provision)? Remember to agree and write a **Development Plan** for the L.E.A., which you can use as a basis for meetings. Contact national S.E.N. organisation for ideas and examples of good practice, and details of local groups.

Copyright Ann Brereton

ADDISS

ADDISS is a national charity offering information, training, resources and support on ADHD a related learning and behavioural difficulties.

Training

We run an annual international 3 day conference.

We offer inset and in-service training for health and education professionals.

We tailor make a training day to suit individual needs.

Resources

We sell a wide range of books and videos by mail order.

We have a resource centre with a large library of materials. The resource centre can be visited to view videos or browse through the information.

Support

We provide support for individual callers who we refer on to their nearest local support group and we also offer support to the 150 support groups across the country.

Newsletter and Subscription

We have a newsletter that goes to individual subscribers and to all the support groups.

Currently ADDISS has the only ADHD Resource Centre in the country. This centre is full of books, videos, articles, etc., and may be visited at any time by appointment. We hope to open to the public full-time in the near future as we have premises on a busy high street.

We have a good working relationship with many professionals across the UK, who have taken advantage of our service and who continue to support us. We work with health professionals, social workers and health visitors to assist in the setting up of local parent support groups.

Contact details
The ADDISS Resource Centre, 10 Station Road, Mill Hilll,
London NW7 2JU.
Tel: 020 8906 9068

Fax: 020 8959 0727
E-mail: info@addiss.co.uk
Website: www.addiss.co.uk

AFASIC

Afasic is the UK charity representing children and young adults with communication impairments, working for their inclusion in society and supporting their parents and carers.

Tony Curtis, UK Director of Development at Afasic, describes how the charity works for children with communication difficulties.

Afasic is the parent-led UK charity representing children and young people with a range of communication impairments – including phonological and articulation difficulties, verbal dyspraxia, dysarthria, semantic pragmatic disorder, Asperger Syndrome and selective mutism. Founded in 1968 by a speech and language therapist, we seek to improve support for children and young people with speech and language impairments and their families by:

- Providing information to parents and carers and professionals
- Offering support at a local level
- Raising awareness of speech and language difficulties
- Lobbying central and local government for improvements in provision
- Promoting good practice.

Information

Parents and carers often feel isolated from support and bereft of information. Afasic's Helpline service is unique. It offers support on all aspects of speech and language impairments – from the nature of impairments to how to choose a school.

The Helpline is supported by a range of publications and by the Afasic website.

In the last year Afasic has published:

- New videos in Urdu and Punjabi, produced by Strathclyde University
- Figures of Speech – a colourful booklet written by students at Moor House School
- Claiming benefits for children with speech and language difficulties.

Going local

Local groups enable parents and carers to support each other – many were first established by speech and language therapists. Local groups also work to enhance vital local services.

Afasic's team of Development Officers in England is involved in a variety of partnerships to raise awareness, improve provision and develop support. Afasic has created over 1500 local training opportunities for parents and professionals in the last twelve months.

Other current projects include:

- A weekly youth club for 11–19 year olds in Redbridge, supported by a youth worker, a speech and language therapist, and volunteers from the speech and language therapy undergraduate course at City University.
- In Tower Hamlets, Afasic's exciting Kheli-Bholi project, which provides to pre-school Bangladeshi children colourful bags full of toys and books which develop their speech and language.
- Singalong booklets produced by Afasic Worcestershire in partnership with Wyre Forest Speech and Language Therapy Department, which will enable parents to share this method of communication with their children.

Spreading the word
Raising awareness of communication difficulties is a key part of Afasic's mission. Examples of our work include:

- Afasic's Glossary Sheets sent to every school in Scotland
- Children with speech and language impairments talking about their educational experience at a conference in Scotland.

Campaigning for better services and for good practice
Some examples of what we do:

- Afasic has urged the Qualifications and Curriculum Authority to make SATs tests more accessible to children with communication difficulties
- In England, Afasic's Development team and the DfES have held a conference to enable therapists and teachers working on the Standards Fund speech and language therapy projects to share experiences and develop models of good practice
- Afasic Scotland, funded by the Scottish Executive, and n partnership with the Dyspraxia Foundation, has produced a dyspraxia training pack, written by Dr Christine Macintyre from Edinburgh University,

which has been distributed to every primary and nursery school in Scotland
• Afasic has met the Education Minister in Northern Ireland to discuss the needs of children with communication difficulties
• In partnership with the British Dyslexia Association, Afasic has launched a training pack to support young children with speech, language and literacy difficulties. The pack has been produced by Janet Wood, Jannet Wright and Joy Stackhouse.

Looking forward

Afasic has exciting plans for the next year:
• workshops, seminars and conferences across the UK
• services, funding permitting, that will support young people with communication impairments as they move from school towards further education, employment and independence
• a renewed presence in Wales and a range of literature in Welsh
• revised publications to reflect changes to the Code of Practice and the SEN Tribunal in England.

Therapists and Afasic

The projects described above show how Afasic often works closely with speech and language therapists to provide high quality and innovative support to children with communication difficulties and their families. Please let us know if you would like to work with us, or if you would like to help us spread the word by giving out our leaflets or displaying our posters. Even better, be part of what we are trying to achieve by becoming a member of Afasic!

Contact details
Afasic
2nd Floor, 50-52 Great Sutton Street, London EC1V ODJ.
Helpline: 08453 55 55 77 (local call rate)
Tel: 020 7490 9410
Fax: 020 7251 2834
E-mail: info(c)afasic.org.uk
Web: http://www.afasic.org.uk

BODY BRUSHING

This therapy involves the use of a small brush to stimulate various specific areas of the body in order to inhibit those reflexes that remain present in spite of age. The condition that results from these uninhibited reflexes is called Discreet Developmental Delay and includes such symptomatic diagnosis as:

1. Gross Motor Dyspraxia
2. Fine Motor Dyspraxia
3. Speech Dyspraxia
4. Attention Deficit Disorder (ADD)
5. Attention Deficit Disorder (Hyperactive) (ADDH)
6. Several Categories of Dyslexia
7. Several Types of Epilepsy
8. Some aspects of Moebius Syndrome
9. Specific Types of ME
10. Oppositional Defiance Disorder
11. Separation Anxiety Disorder

And also many types of mono-phobic, multi-phobic and tree floating anxiety disorders.

This effective and internationally recognised Therapy was pioneered by Steve Clarke. Steve has been developing and refining his techniques continually since the late 1980s, and has trained therapists in his work and many others in the techniques of screening for the initial detection of the condition.

Testimonials to the success of the work are continually being made, and Steve travels each month to U.S.A., Brazil, France and Ireland as well as holding clinics in various Centres round the U.K.

Procedure

Once an Initial Consultation has determined that aberrant reflexes might be present a full Diagnostic Assessment takes place to determine the stage at which Development has been delayed. This process will take around 2 hours.

The results of the D.A. are sent in a Report to the parents, and if the Therapy is deemed appropriate, that is meeting all of several requisites, the treatment begins.

Consultations

Once a month until a period of consolidation or rest is allowed which may be for 1 to 6 months.

The same battery of tests is carried out each time, allowing for accurate assessment of progress.

The parents or carers are shown one or two very precise 'brushings' to do every day, twice a day. These will take on average 10 minutes each time.

The Rationale

In normal development three sets of reflexes appear, stay for a while then inhibit as a result of stimulation and usage
• Foetal Reflexes, developing as early as a few weeks after conception
• Primitive or survival Reflexes, present at or around birth and seem to either facilitate birth, or help the newborn to survive the critical 3 to 4 months after birth
• Infant or transitory Reflexes, developing around 5 months after birth and persisting up to 11 to 14 months of age.

The fourth set of Reflexes the Posturals, start to develop from birth, and we retain them in their full form for life.

One example – the baby startle reflex – the Moro, is responsible for massive outpourings of adrenaline. If the Moro is still present in an older child then this surplus of adrenaline will produce hyper-activity. We need it to be inhibited.

The results of a programme of Body Brushing on a child can be spectacular.

Contact details
Murdo White.
Tel: 01568 612153

THE BROXBOURNE DYSLEXIA UNIT

The Broxbourne Dyslexia Unit has been in existence for 16 years and over that time has built up a relationship with the LEA and many local schools, who have come to appreciate and trust our diagnostic teaching assessments as valid and helpful signposts in the process of giving help to children, and adults, who are having problems with literacy. The aim of our assessments is not too put a 'label' on a difficulty, but to tease out the strengths and weaknesses of a person's learning style and then to make suggestions for how to help. Sometimes the diagnosis is clear and a dyslexic pattern emerges; sometimes we suggest referral to other experts, optometrists, dyspraxia practitioners, speech therapists or to a paediatrician if we think there is a medical difficulty.

We give detailed suggestions for help within the school, from class and subject teachers and LSAs, and also at home. Sometimes it is appropriate to suggest some one-to-one teaching from a specialist. We try to arrange this but it is increasingly difficult to find teachers with vacancies.

The Unit runs training courses for the OCR diploma and certificate and also for classroom assistants. Our aim is to give knowledge to schools so that they can become 'dyslexia friendly'. We also run Saturday courses each term on dyslexia associated specific difficulties. We have a large selection of books and materials for sale.

In all these ways we are trying to raise awareness and to promulgate 'best practice'.

Contact details
The Broxbourne Dyslexia Unit, The Priests' House, 90 High Street, Broxbourne, Herts EN10 7DZ
Tel: 01992 442002

EDUCATIONAL KINESIOLOGY EMBRACING BRAIN GYM®

Today's complex learning environment causes some children (and adults) to either switch off or become disruptive due to their inability to cope with incoming stimuli. These people are often labelled as 'day dreaming', 'not concentrating', 'lazy', 'deBant', 'uncooperative', 'dyslexic', 'trouble-maker' or 'ADD' despite constant efforts by the child, parents and teachers.

When a student fails to benefit from conventional teaching strategies, then it is time to examine the person's neurology to see if there is a physical basis underlying his poor academic performance. We must check to see if the person can control and voluntarily direct his or her responses or see if they are still governed by primitive patterns of response, which permit him to have only immature reactions, which interfere with the higher more complex skills.

We do not (yet) understand (fully) why one child finds an activity simple whilst another finds the same activity difficult. Through research we have discovered that the 'wiring' in the brain is unique for each person.

Although Brain Gym is valuable in itself, the process can be achieved more quickly with a balance from an Educational Kinesiology (Edu-K) practitioner, which is then followed by a series of specific Brain Gym activities practised daily for a few weeks to consolidate the changes made during the balance.

Childhood Reflexes

The retention of primitive baby reflexes is the underlying cause of many learning and behavioural problems. When these reflexes do not inhibit as expected and remain active in a person's system, they are the underlying causes of many learning and behavioural problems in childhood and adulthood such as hyperactivity, dyslexia, disruptive behaviour and poor memory, lack of concentration and co-ordination.

Twelve of the Childhood Reflexes known to medicine are:

• Fear Paralysis Reflex – causes the child to feel overwhelmed or fearful or both and may result in depression, excessive shyness or elective mutism.
• Moro Reflex – can have a major effect on behaviour, emotions and stress levels.

- Tonic Labyrinthine Reflex – has a major effect on learning and co-ordination.
- Palmar Reflex – affects children's handwriting abilities and pencil grip.
- Infant Plantar Reflex – can affect smooth running and walking.
- Asymmetrical Tonic Neck Reflex – affects handwriting abilities and pencil grip.
- Babinski Reflex – can contribute to feet problems.
- Symmetrical Tonic Neck Reflex – will cause a child to slump when sitting, especially at a table or desk,
- Vestibular Reflex – is often related to auditory confusion and delay, Attention Deficit Disorder (ADD) or Attention Deficit and Hyperactive Disorder (ADHD) or both.
- Ocular Motor Reflex – affects reading and writing.

Inappropriate Retention of Primitive Reflexes
If primitive reflexes are still inappropriately retained within a person's system, this causes developmental delay. But this can be corrected by using Brain Gym®, Vision gym™ and Edu-K techniques and procedures to improve the processing of sensory information. Thus a child develops more mature patterns of response, so making it easier to learn academic skills such as reading, writing, spelling and maths.

Fifty years ago, Dyspraxia was unheard of; even if there were a few fidgety children (in the classroom). The number of children today who have learning problems is increasing. Whether this is due to our lifestyles or the environment has yet to be decided, but we do know that these children need help.

Acknowledgements
We acknowledge gratefully the contribution on Inappropriately Retained Primitive Reflexes from Jenny Blumsom, whose Edu-K practice is in Hertfordshire, who has drawn heavily on the research and practice of Claire Hocking, a Brain Gym Instructor and Educational Kinesiologist, practising in Wendouree, Victoria Australia.

Bibliography
A full bibliography on Educational Kinesiology, Brain Gym and Childhood Reflexes can be obtained from the Educational Kinesiology

(UK) Foundation, 12 Golden Rise, Hendon, London NW4 2HR (e-mail ekukf@mccarrol.dircon.co.uk).

Contact details
Jenny Blumsom PgDipMIPD
Educational Kinesiology and Counselling
23 The Gardens, Brookmans Park, Hatfield, Herts AL9 7UL.
Tel: (answerphone) 01707 645000
E-mail: jennyblumsom@nigelbain.cix.co.uk

BRITISH DYSLEXIA ASSOCIATION

How parents can help

Your child is failing at school. He was the first to know it but he does not know how to help himself and he cannot explain his difficulties. The longer he goes unaided the more difficult the problem becomes.

1. *Be positive*

Consider carefully his strengths and his weaknesses and find out all you can about the reasons for his non-achievement, and ways of alleviating it. Discuss the problem with his teacher and with him. Urgently and determinedly seek appropriate assessment of his difficulties and appropriate teaching help. Both parents need to be involved in all consultations, etc. But, please, do not hawk him round for assessment at short intervals by a variety of experts. Find the person in whom you have faith and stick with him.

2. *Be patient and persevering*

(a) Be patient and persevering with his teachers – carefully develop a good parent–teacher relationship. You must set up the communication network and keep it going. Information is not always passed on from teacher to teacher or school to school.

If a new teacher arrives, go and make yourself known to him. At secondary level you need to get to know the year tutor or house master and all subject teachers.

Be diplomatic – of course you are very worried and anxious (teachers should understand this – but they also have problems – a whole class full). At all times ask yourself 'Is what I am doing helping my child or merely giving vent to my own frustration?' Keep your anger and your bitterness to yourself, whatever anyone says to you or about you. Your attitude can do more harm than good, so keep cool, calm and dignified.

(b) Be patient and persevering with him – patiently teach him to do things for himself; to tie his tie (do this over his shoulder in front of the mirror), tie his shoe laces, to dress himself correctly, to tell the time, left from right, etc. Be patient also with the progress he makes once he is receiving appropriate teaching help – no miracles will happen; it takes time, determination and hard work.

Teach him independence and how to help himself. For example, until he knows left from right, see that his bicycle bell is on the left handle bar so that he can ride on the bell side of the road. Send him on simple errands, encourage him to use the telephone, particularly the public phone. If he has a train journey to make alone, tell him what time he should arrive and how many stops there will be before his destination.

3. Be aware

Be aware of the problems, symptoms and signs of stress. He will be called 'dumb head', etc. by his peers, 'lazy', 'stupid' by some adults; he will be late to football or miss it altogether because he has not finished his written work, and it takes him so long to change and get his boots on. He will hate the teacher who asks him to read in front of the class or holds him up to ridicule for the results of a multiplication tables or a spelling test. He will be frustrated by so many things besides school work – not comprehending the time of year in relation to the months, not knowing which day of the week it is, not being able to differentiate between his nearest local towns.

He has many disappointments, but he learns to live with them and can be helped to avoid them most of the time – providing you can be one step ahead and realise the risk before it becomes a problem – and do something about it.

Be aware of stress signs, such as bed-wetting and introversion which need subtle handling. Aggression and anti-social behaviour have to be checked gently but firmly. Never think all the stress signs are because he is dyslexic – he is growing up too and has all the problems of adolescence. It is a good idea to talk to parents of non-dyslexic children – how are they behaving? It helps to get things into perspective.

Be aware also of the ignorance and misunderstanding you will meet at all levels. Head teachers, teachers, G.P.s, psychologists, employers, etc. – not all, by any stretch of the imagination, have understanding or sympathy for the dyslexic.

It follows therefore that not all the advice you are given is good advice.

Again, be aware that school failure is often more obvious at home. You have to decide when he is twisting you round his little finger and when the problems are overwhelming him. You need to be something of a psychologist. 'I'm dyslexic – I can't do it'. 'Yes, you're dyslexic and it will take you longer; you know that, but you can do it'. Sometimes they may try it on – don't encourage it! This is where the good parent–teacher relationship comes into its own. The teacher in whom you have confidence will be able to put your mind at rest or take action appropriately.

Are you aware that your child has to work exceedingly hard at school and does get very, very tired? He may even become so exhausted he needs a day off occasionally. So avoid pressure at home with reading and writing. Even though they forget a lot during school holidays – let them have holidays. Other things to avoid – jealousies between siblings. Your dyslexic child (or children) is very dependent on you and you give him a great deal of your attention. But it must never be at the expense of other children in the family who appear to be doing well without any help from you. They can develop all sorts of emotional problems through feeling left out and jealous and you may not see it happening. Never fall into the trap of comparing one child with another either in or out of your family.

Avoid failure situations at home – he gets enough of those at school. Home must be a safe place, so do not show your anxiety if you can possibly avoid it – it adds to his feeling of inadequacy. You are in danger of becoming neurotic and of being over protective. At some stage mothers of dyslexics will doubtless succumb to this – but make it as short as possible and then get things back into perspective. Generally men, whilst finding it difficult to accept that their child has a specific problem, are more objective and no-one calls them 'neurotic mothers'. So life is considerably easier for everyone if the family is involved and not just mother and child, and emotional situations within the home are less likely to arise. Of course, mother and father will not always agree as to the best course of action – this is normal.

4. Be practical

Not many parents are able to teach their own children, but there are many ways in which you can help, unobtrusively.

Read to him – never mind his age. Up to 5, 6, 7 you will be doing this anyway - do not ask him to, but let him if he wants to. He may ask you to at 15, 16, 17. There is a lot of reading to be done, and many dyslexics find that after a while they are no longer comprehending what they are reading - that is when you come in. Even so, he may only be able to take in so much before his concentration goes, so it has to be done in short spells.

Note-taking is difficult – particularly copying from the blackboard. Writing deteriorates and words are sometimes omitted (leaving out 'not' or 'no' makes a vast difference to the sense of a sentence). So suggest you type his notes.

His English Literature set books can be put on tape – it takes time. You may find they are already on cassettes. Take him to his Shakespeare play: listen to it on the radio.

There is a huge variety of things to be learned from the television – watch it with him and discuss what you see. There are endless games to play, involving the whole family or just a couple of you, which will help him.

It is vital to keep him motivated – build on his strengths – he has some and they need encouraging. Encourage his interests and feed him information. Encourage leisure activities – fishing, collecting stamps or fossils, modelling, cooking, etc. Give praise – take no achievement for granted – a slight improvement in handwriting – when he lays the table correctly, etc. It is all too easy to complain – it is far more difficult to remember to praise and we all need encouragement.

Boost his self-confidence and self-esteem. Even if he appears self-assured, deep down he is very anxious.

Jennifer Smith

Contact details
British Dyslexia Association
98 London Rd, READING RG1 5AU.
Helpline: 0118 968 8271
Fax: 0118 935 1927
E-mail (Helpline): info@dyslexiahelp-bda.demon.co.uk
Web: http://www.bda-dyslexia.org.uk/

DAVIS® DYSLEXIA CORRECTION PROGRAMME

Ronald D. Davis believes dyslexia to be a gift rather than a disability; many famous people are dyslexic and they are gifted in art, science, sports, business or politics, such as Leonardo da Vinci, Einstein, Steven Redgrave, Richard Branson or Winston Churchill. Dyslexics are usually highly intelligent, but many often fail to achieve their promise at school. The Davis Dyslexia Programme aims to correct rather than cure dyslexia and thereby help dyslexics achieve more.

The cornerstone of Davis' approach is the discovery that dyslexia and many other learning disabilities come from a perceptual talent and not from brain damage or deficit. He has found that dyslexics mentally perceive things in three dimensions and can easily alter their perspective. This is known as 'moving the mind's eye' and is often associated with imagination. Davis has described this process as 'becoming disorientated' and how a dyslexic becomes disorientated when trying to read or write. To solve this, they develop coping solutions and habits that may prevent successful learning in the future. Ironically, dyslexics use this disorientation when they are being highly creative, intuitive and insightful. The Davis approach is to help the individual recognise and control this disorientation, and thereby learn to achieve their academic promise, without losing the ability to be creative and imaginative.

The Davis Dyslexia Programme is provided as an intensive corrective programme for adults and children aged 8 and over. The process starts with a consultation where the student, the parent and the Davis Facilitator carry out an assessment and decide if the programme is appropriate. Each programme is geared to the student's individual needs. It is vital for the participants to 'buy in' to the programme before starting.

This assessment is followed by a 30 hour intensive programme, which includes Davis Orientation Counselling, Davis Symbol Mastery and Coordination Training. For example, Symbol Mastery involves the student in developing their own images of words and concepts using clay to make the models. Students and parents are taught reading techniques such as Spell-Reading, Picture at Punctuation and Sweep-Sweep-Spelll. These techniques are described in Ronald D. Davis' book, *The Gift of Dyslexia*. Once the basic reading correction techniques are learned, the programme moves on to teaching the mastery of specific terms that the individual needs to be able to function in school.

These may lead on further to learning mathematical concepts if required.

The programme is concluded by the Facilitator, student and parent or tutor developing a Home Study Programme which gives the student a number of tasks and exercises to carry out over the following months. We provide the pack of materials to support this programme. For example, there is a list of 'trigger words' that must be learned using the Symbol Mastery techniques using clay. The parent or tutor will be taught how to be a coach to provide day to day support and the Facilitator will provide a limited amount of follow up as part of the programme.

Individuals who have been labelled as having Attention Deficit Disorder (ADD) or Attention Deficit Hyperactivity Disorder (ADHD) may also have these problems and can also benefit from this programme.

Developing academic skills

Dyslexics can develop their academic skills by applying a number of approaches:

• Encourage the use of pictures to illustrate words and mind mapping – dyslexics are predominantly visual thinkers who find visual images easier to understand than written words. They need to be able to create pictures from the meaning of the word, associating concepts and related words with the written word.

• Make learning sessions as interesting and fun as possible – this will help them in focusing and make it less likely that they will appear inattentive and fidget. It is possible to ask them to verify that they have learned and memorised concepts by asking them to explain them verbally.

• Use Symbol Mastery with their Coach to learn specific words that cause them to disorientate or trigger. This involves clay modelling, using a dictionary and discussing the concept of the word in an interesting and enjoyable way that gives the word meaning and helps recall for written work. This will usually avoid similar problems once words are mastered in this way.

• Ensure that they understand what they need to focus on when writing – such as one of content, grammar or presentation. They can often write accurately and neatly when not under time pressure and with topics they find interesting and stimulating (sciences, technology and the environment).

Dyslexics are often self confident in most situations, except when disoriented, confused or under pressure. They can develop self-confidence in their own ability when building on achievement or partial achievement of difficult areas (spelling, accurate sentence construction, correct grammar, trigger words) and thereby reduce the number of situations causing disorientation and hence poor written work. There are some good tips in the article at: http://www.dyslexia.com/library/classroom.htm.

Contact details
Dyslexia Correction Centre, Holtwood, Brockenhurst Road,
Ascot SL5 9HA
Tel: 01344 622115
E-mail: dyslexia@btinternet.com
Web: www.dyslexia.com

THE DYSLEXIA INSTITUTE

The Dyslexia Institute (DI) is an educational charity, founded in 1972, for the assessment and teaching of people with dyslexia and training for specialist teachers. It has grown to become the only national dyslexia teaching organisation in the world.

It provides a national network of 25 main centres and some 145 linked learning centres, offering individual assessments by Chartered Psychologists and qualified Teacher Assessors and screening for schools, colleges and other organisations. Tuition is provided in literacy, mathematics and study skills using our own highly successful teaching methods and materials. Our Teacher Training Service offers regionally based Short Courses on dyslexia and literacy. Postgraduate Diplomas and Postgraduate Certificates (the Certificate is available by distance learning) validated by the University of York are also offered. An accredited Teaching Assistants course is being introduced during 2002.

The DI carries out over 7000 assessments each year and currently provides specialist tuition for over 3000 children in its Centres, outposts and school units. The effectiveness of DI teaching methods and materials has been warmly praised by thousands of grateful children and their parents. It is dependent upon fees from assessments, tuition and teacher training courses and from the sale of resources and publications. In recent years its research programme has benefited from grants from the National lotteries Charities Board and from the DfES, and its Training Service has been supported by the Teacher Training Agency. The DI and the DI Bursary Fund also greatly benefit from the donations, both large and small, from business, trusts and individuals.

Teaching at the DI is highly structured, with progress made in small steps, building on what has gone before. It is multi-sensory in that it uses as many channels as possible to promote memory, with the stronger senses supporting the weaker ones. The teaching uses a phonic approach that helps the student to understand the logical structure of written language. Twice a year parents receive progress reports and at least once a year, parents' evenings are held.

Contact details
The Dyslexia Institute
Park House, Wick Road, Egham, Surrey TW20 0HH.
Tel: 01784 222300   Fax: 01784 222333

DDAT
A REMARKABLE DISCOVERY OF 'HOPE' FOR THOSE SUFFERING FROM LEARNING DIFFICULTIES

Background

Research into the underlying cause of learning difficulties has been contentious for many years. Various theories have been put forward, but none has had any significant impact on the removal of the essential symptoms of the problem. Far too many people still suffer from poor concentration, difficulties with reading, difficulties with comprehension, coordination problems, self esteem, etc.

One theory that has been around for many years (although disregarded by the vast majority in the 'Dyslexia Industry') is the cerebella–vestibular theory. Essentially this says that the sensory inputs from the vestibular into the cerebellum are not appropriately used and this causes the cerebellum to not fulfil its function in assisting the thinking brain in the process of 'learning'.

With advice from Professor Rod Nicolson and Dr Angela Fawcett of Sheffield University, UK, DDAT has put together a testing and remediation programme that is showing remarkable results. Despite the research programme being less than 3 years old, already large numbers of lives have been changed and substantial research data collected demonstrating that it is feasible, without drugs, to deal with the underlying cause of the problem.

The extent of the problem

One of several remarkable things about this whole programme is the discovery of the real extent of those suffering from learning difficulties. Because of science being so misunderstood, the vast majority of those and who underachieve simply accept it as a problem that cannot be resolved. Now we are starting to describe the symptoms and the potential results, we discover that huge numbers of folk live with these symptoms every day of their lives. In the studies done within schools we often find that between 15 and 20 percent of all children are affected and that they can have their effectiveness dramatically increased in a matter of months.

The ease of achieving the solution

Another remarkable factor is that these results can be achieved without the use of drugs. Patients wishing to go through the programme are tested for the effectiveness of their cerebellum and a series of exercises appropriate to the needs are prescribed for them. Every six weeks their progress is monitored and the exercise regime adjusted until their symptoms have subsided. This typically takes between 5 and 9 months. The exercises are conducted twice every day and take only 5 to 10 minutes.

Not only are the academic symptoms improving (reading, hand-writing, spelling, etc) but also self esteem is seen to improve very dramatically. Anecdotally, reports of large number of other improvements – all of which are scientifically logical but not yet scientifically measured and reported (these include travel sickness, sporting ability, etc).

The potential for this remediation

Obviously the implications for education and all the impact upon people's lives are stunning. When you consider that it is well known that a large proportion of the criminal population suffers from learning difficulties – it is difficult to comprehend the kind of social impact that would be had if as a matter of course criminals were put through such a programme. A study in a British jail starts in a few weeks' time to measure the impact of this.

Other research projects include the potential impact on adult literacy, depression, suicidal tendencies, homeless, bullying, long term unemployed, etc. It is strongly suspected but not yet proven that all of these groups include a significant proportion of people whose lives have been frustrated by the underachievement caused directly from their learning difficulties. Studies in all these areas are being planned to start within the coming months.

DDAT's vision

DDAT's role has been to carry out action based research to demonstrate and measure the progress achievable. This will continue – and to collect the data a number of private clinics have been opened in the UK. A pilot clinic has also been opened in Sydney, Australia, to start the development of all the technical and training programmes necessary to roll out centres world-wide. The next area to be opened up is North America where 15 clinics were planned during 2003.

Whilst all these clinics are 'private clinics', work has been taking place for the last 18 months on the development of equipment and training programmes that de-skill the remediation to enable it to be taken into schools by education boards thus making it available to all – including those who are unable to pay for the treatment.

Wynford Dore

Contact details
DDAT.
Tel: 0870 737 0017
Web: http://www.ddat.co.uk

THE HELEN ARKELL DYSLEXIA CENTRE

The Helen Arkell Dyslexia Centre (HADC) believes that anyone with dyslexia deserves the expert assessment and tuition we can provide regardless of the ability to pay.

HADC offers help and advice in every aspect of recognising and supporting dyslexic people.

HADC is the oldest established dyslexia centre in the UK, founded by Helen Arkell in 1971.

HADC is proud of its high professional reputation.

How do we do this?

Having a team of over 150 experienced professionals means we can offer a wide range of services to dyslexic people, their families, and to professionals seeking training and advice.

For dyslexic people and their families we offer:

- Consultations – an initial full discussion of problems with advice on the way forward
- Assessments – from a wide range of professionals ensuring the 'right fit'
- Specialist tuition – one on one or small group, this is always 'individualised'
- Short courses including summer schools for a booster in skills and confidence
- Speech and language therapy where needed
- Adult Literary Group.

For professionals we offer:
- OCR professional training courses to Diploma level
- Short courses to update and learn new methods and strategies
- Conferences – at least one annually
- Inservice sessions in schools and businesses to increase awareness and create dyslexia friendly classrooms and work environments
- Specialist bookshop with a mail order facility.

Our donors also enable us to create effective partnerships in projects which can have far reaching effects for large numbers of dyslexic people. In recent years these have focused on schools, colleges, Local Education Authorities and the prison service.

In all our services we retain a personal, friendly approach; a high level of professionalism; and seek the best solution for each individual or organisation.

Contact details
Helen Arkell Dyslexia Centre, Frensham, Farnham, Surrey GU10 3BW.
Tel: 01252 792400
E-mail: enquiries@arkellcentre.org.uk
Website: www.arkellcentre.org.uk

HORNSBY INTERNATIONAL DYSLEXIA CENTRE

The Hornsby Centre is one of the world's leading specialist dyslexia centres. The Centre aims to educate, advise, assist and support teachers and parents in helping the dyslexic individual.

We provide first class training courses for teachers, other professionals and parents by attendance at the centre in London or via Distance Learning. Short courses include the foundation course, which provides a general overview and understanding of dyslexia and the study skills course, which enables adults to support children in reaching their full potential.

For teachers who wish to advance their knowledge of Specific Learning Difficulties, we offer the OCR Certificate and OCR Diploma. We also run our own Hornsby Certificate and Diploma courses. The Diploma is an open entry course, providing training for both teachers and those who wish to work with dyslexics but who do not have qualified teacher status.

Students on the longer-term Hornsby courses undertake teaching practice at local primary schools with pupils who are experiencing literacy difficulties. In the last year we have also established a weekly learners' group called the Smart Club. The Club runs on Tuesday and Wednesday evenings for a small group of primary children from the local area who are experiencing literacy difficulties.

The Hornsby Diploma by Distance Learning allows individuals to study at their own pace, at any location. Since the course began, students from 60 different countries have completed the Diploma.

In addition to the training courses we run, we provide other services at the centre. Educational assessments by chartered psychologists and specialist teachers are available and also the provision of concession certificates for external examinations.

We are able to provide a list of qualified tutors for a small administration fee.

We have a Bookshop at the centre, stocking a wide range of workbooks, textbooks, computer software and teaching materials. Resources may be purchased in person, by telephone, mail order or the Internet.

The centre has a membership scheme, called the Friends of the Hornsby Centre. The Friends started in 1991 when students on Hornsby courses felt there was a need to keep in touch and up to date with the centre. Friends receive a newsletter each term, keeping them up to date with the latest developments in SpLD, news of current and forthcoming events and the work at the Centre. Up-date conferences are held three times a year, providing well-known guest speakers. Topics covered are of current concern, progress in research and the problems of teaching specific subjects. The conferences are also good social occasions offering the opportunity to meet others with similar interests.

Contact details
The Hornsby International Dyslexia Centre
Wye Street, London SW II 2HB.
Tel: 020 7223 1144
Fax: 020 7924 1112
E-mail: dyslexia@hornsby.co.uk
Web: http://www.hornsby.co.uk

SPELL

Although claims are made by exponents of various treatments and therapies that they have life-long impact, in most cases there is no research evidence to support the claims. Currently neither The National Autistic Society (NAS) nor any Local Education Authority has made a commitment to any particular treatment or therapy.

Parents and professionals are encouraged to investigate thoroughly all approaches available in order to determine which might be appropriate for any one individual based on his or her needs.

What is the SPELL approach?

Over the past few years the educational approach of the NAS schools and adult centre has concentrated on specific programmes to reduce the effects of the impairments of imagination, communication and social skills that underlie autism. This is in addition to the generally accepted emphasis on structure, consistency, reduction of disturbing stimuli and a high degree of organisation.

Within the NAS services every minute of every day is recognised as a learning opportunity. Staff working collaboratively design education and care plans which encompass the 24 hours of the day for children in residential settings.

The acronym used to describe this approach is SPELL:

Structure
Positive
Empathetic
Low arousal
Links

SPELL

The approach addresses the needs for the child with autism to have continuity and order in his or her life. The child needs to be able to predict events, and his or her environment needs to be modified sufficiently to reduce anxiety.

It has been developed to overcome or reduce the disabling effects of autism by providing a broad and balanced curriculum which gives extra help in the area of impairments.

Structure
Structure helps with organisation and making sense of what can be a very confusing world. It can help provide a safer world by the removal or reduction of unexpected or unpredictable events.

Positive
Positive attitudes and appropriate expectations (not so high as to cause anxiety, and not so low as to cause boredom) aim to enhance the child's self confidence and self esteem. We design education programmes that intervene in the child's autism aiming to maximise and build on strengths.

Empathetic
Seeing the world from the child's unique viewpoint, and aiming to understand his or her perceptions demands empathy and uses the teacher's skills in designing a differential programme which starts from the position of the individual child.

Low arousal
The classroom and care setting needs to be calm and focused, allowing opportunities for relaxation and relief of tension. Clutter and distraction may be inhibiting, and a low arousal setting is likely to be most reassuring. We make use of physical education and a variety of relaxation techniques to maintain an ordered and harmonious atmosphere.

Our style is essentially non-confrontational, and, through supported rehearsal, students are encouraged to try new and potentially aversive experiences thereby grow in confidence.

Links
It is vital that we communicate effectively with parents, other schools and agencies. In order to maximise the children's opportunities for inclusion in mainstream schools we access the National Curriculum and aim to maintain all the vital links with the community.

The National Curriculum
The National Curriculum is often decried as being of no use to children with severe disabilities, but with imaginative application even the most

ethereal of subjects can be modified and adapted to ensure relevant and enjoyable programmes of education. For example, Art can be linked to Geography, Science and Mathematics. Children with a flair for numbers can have those skills extended within areas of curricular relevance and long-term practical application. Some subjects in the National Curriculum can be used directly to address the triad of impairments. For example, children with autistic spectrum disorders have difficulty with hypothesising and predicting. Subjects such as Science can provide opportunities for them to explore these areas in a safe but challenging way.

SPELL enables the trained observer to analyse the education environment and to assist in the creation of a setting where the child with an autistic spectrum disorder can learn.

SPELL, as an approach, is still in the developing stages. As such, it is continually being monitored and assessed.

TEACCH

The TEACCH (Treatment and Education of Autistic and Related Communication Handicapped Children) approach, from the University of North Carolina, has been successfully adapted for use in the NAS schools and operates in conjunction with our own methods. If you would like to receive information on TEACCH please contact the NAS Information Centre on the telephone number below.

The NAS Information Centre

The NAS Information Centre produces fact sheets on a wide variety of topics and can provide customised reference lists in response to individual requests. The lists are extracted from our database which contains over 11000 books and articles from the autism field. This service is particularly useful for those wanting to research a specific subject thoroughly.

If you require information on other approaches please contact the NAS Information Centre at the London address.

Contact details

The National Autistic Society,
393 City Road, London EC1V 1NG, UK.
Helpline: 0845 070 4004

Tel: 020 7833 2299
Fax: 020 7833 9666
E-mail: nas@nas.org.uk;
Web: http://www.nas.org.uk

If you require advice on educational matters, write to: Richard Mills, NAS Services Division, Church House, Church Road, Filton, Bristol BS34 78D.

If you require information on training contact:
NAS Training Services Department
4th Floor, Castle Heights, 72 Maid Marian Way
Nottingham NGI 6BJ.
Tel: 0115 911 3363
Fax: 0115 911 3362
E-mail: training@nas.org.uk

THE INSTITUTE FOR NEURO-PHYSIOLOGICAL PSYCHOLOGY

NEURO-DEVELOPMENTAL DELAY (NDD) is often found to be a vital 'missing link' to Dyslexia, Dyspraxia, ADD/ADHD, Behavioural difficulties, Frustration, Exhaustion, etc.

NDD is an under-functioning in the central nervous system, which means that the neurological responses which should link the body and brain <u>automatically</u> do not function efficiently. All our responses are based on information received through our senses – i.e. sight, hearing, taste, smell, touch, and movement around us. This information should then be automatically 'processed' in the appropriate parts of the brain speedily and efficiently in order to allow us to function effectively and harmoniously. In this way our <u>Sensory</u> and <u>Motor</u> Systems become integrated.

These neurological responses are known as **Primitive** and **Postural Neurological Reflexes**, and they can be tested and measured to ascertain their effectiveness. In a 'normal' baby, the brain's neural clock determines correct timing such that appropriate development of the Reflexes and associated 'developmental milestones are achieved from the moment of conception through to approximately 2 years of age, by which time the Reflexes should have reached full maturation (with a few exceptions). Therefore, within this time we can observe all babies going through various standard patterns of movement and development, e.g. initially a floppy reflexive mass that reacts automatically to basic needs – sucking for feeding, crying if uncomfortable, etc. It then develops the ability to make <u>deliberate movements</u>, such as rolling over, crawling on the tummy and then crawling on hands and knees, before finally defeating gravity and standing upright, etc. These latter movements are <u>Postural Reflexes</u> that allow the child to adapt to his environment and develop his <u>Perceptual</u> and <u>Conceptual Systems</u> that are required for <u>all later learning</u>. Movement is vital for all learning to take place. Sometimes some of these Reflex areas of development are curtailed or totally missed out, resulting in missing links in the system.

No-one has a perfect system, but the body should be able to compensate for any of these little missing links in the system that might have occurred during the development process. However, if there is too large a cluster of aberrant (incorrect) Reflexes, then the system becomes overloaded, which then results in repercussions in both physical and psychological or behavioural areas, also <u>adversely affecting academic functioning to a greater or lesser extent</u>.

Restoring the Link

The Remediation Therapy lies in a programme of specialised slow movements, known as 'The Home Programme'. These slow movements, which take approximately 10 minutes daily, are designed to correct the deficiencies in the baby's neural clock, i.e. to give the child a 'second chance' so as to mend the missing links in the system.

Through the Home Programme therefore, the body and brain are given the opportunity to learn to develop <u>automatic</u> neurological reflex response proprioceptively, i.e. through the <u>movement</u> of muscles and joints. In this way muscle <u>compensation</u> is no longer required, thus more energy is available, and stress and fatigue are decreased. The central nervous system 'calms down' and body functioning becomes more fluid and efficient, thus laying the <u>VITAL 'STRUCTURAL FOUNDATIONS'</u> for multi-sensory teaching methods to be processed efficiently.

Result…a happy, confident child, able to succeed – **'Link Restored'**.

Contact details
Gill Geraerts NDT
The Institute for Neuro-Physiological Psychology.
Tel: 01582 766797

THE SPECIALIST OPTOMETRIST AND DYSLEXIA

If you suspect you child is having reading difficulties, it is advised that you see an Optometrist. It is important to find one who specialises in this field, ideally through recommendation.

It may seem obvious, but we, as Optometrists, still get children brought to us who have struggled for years with their reading and who are simply in need of spectacles. For example, although long-sighted children are able to do close work, it requires greater effort and is harder to sustain. When the effort becomes too much, the words may blur or move about making reading more difficult. Nowadays, children do not always have eye checks at school, and when they do some defects are not always apparent.

There is also a significant proportion of children whose eyes fail to work together correctly. A very common problem is poor convergence. When we read, our eyes have to converge so that the brain receives two matching images. When double vision is demonstrated to the child, it is not unusual for them to recognise it as frequently experienced. This is a condition that can usually be cured with a short intensive course of simple exercises. Similarly, some children have poor general control of their eye muscles. This is often a problem for the Dyspraxic child or one with general poor muscle tone and can result in poor tracking. This is an inability to follow along a line of print smoothly with both eyes. In such cases, eye exercises can usually be beneficial.

When all conventional investigations have been done, and any associated problems eliminated, then the use of colour will be considered. In some individuals, colour has been shown to make a substantial difference to the way they perceive the written page. Words that previously appeared to run together, move about, or form odd patterns on the page can appear normal, thus enabling the individual to read. During investigation, various coloured overlays are applied to a page of text in order to establish whether they may be beneficial. The Optometrist can then check for improvement in the rate and fluency of the reading to assess whether this approach is worth pursuing. It is recommended that the appropriate colour be used as an overlay for approximately one school term before investigations are done with the 'Intuitive Colorimeter'. This machine enables the exact colour for spectacles to be determined. It has been suggested that children may reject the idea of wearing coloured spectacles in school. However, experience has shown that they generally wear their 'magic glasses' with pride!

It is important to be aware that only a small proportion of Dyslexics are likely benefit from colour. Additionally, for children under 7 the examination may have to be simplified. In such cases, some tests might have to be postponed to a later date, and results may not be as comprehensive. A conventional eye examination is recommended to all children as they start school, especially those who have a relative with a squint or 'lazy eye'. This basic eye examination is covered by the N.H.S., but unfortunately more extensive investigation into reading difficulties will not be.

Whatever the specific nature of your child's problem, an Optometrist might be able to help, and intervention could lead to a significant improvement in reading age.

Contact details
Institute of Optometry.
Tel: 020 7407 4183

THE SUNFLOWER METHOD

Summary

The Sunflower Trust helps children with learning difficulties to perform better, achieve more and enjoy more fruitful, socially integrated lives. The Sunflower Method uses a combination of natural health treatments to normalise many aspects of functional neurology in ways that are measured and matched individually to each child.

The assessment of the functional neurology involves a series of screening procedures which broadly fall into four areas, as follows:

1. The assessment and treatment of a child's musculo skeletal system in relation to the muscle balance and coordination.
2. The assessment and treatment of fine reflex systems relating to eyes, ears, balance, and coordination as mediated by the vestibular mechanism and associated with left and right coordination and brain activity.
3. The assessment of the functional state of many biological pathways using biomarkers. This includes all the basic support systems— digestion, respiration, detoxification, glandular, autoimmune, plus allergies and sensitivities, with reference to the biochemical pathways that are found to be out of balance. A whole range of nutritional co-factors relevant to the particular pathways found are tested and the appropriate prescriptions given. Dietary supplements and modification may be used when appropriate.
4. The assessment of the child to challenges of the kind that are a part of every-day life and education are measured and re-patterned in way that enables the child to communicate more fully with his abilities, rather than his vulnerabilities.

One of the basic principles underlying the Sunflower Method is that the nervous system, autoimmune and autonomic nervous systems are integrated with the motor sensory system. The neurological aspects of each child at the hypothalamic area of the brain and at the level of the neurotransmitters that regulate the behaviour of each cell of the body are unseparable. They operate and integrate collectively and in a holographic manner. To separate out different elements of these systems and their effects on each other is a fragmented and inefficient approach to healthcare, even though specialists of all kinds may deal with a part of the picture. The ecological approach using integrated natural medicine in a systematic and measurable way, enables each child to make big changes safely and quickly with little risk of damage or disruption for a minimum expenditure of time and money.

There is a lot of evidence to support the value of the various natural treatments employed, including osteopathy, homeopathy, acupuncture without needles, nutritional medicine and neuro linguistic programming, when these are used together in an integrated way by specially trained and professionally qualified practitioners.

Conclusion

Most new breakthroughs are not necessarily radical in themselves but involve using existing knowledge and technology in new ways that are less cumbersome, safer and more efficient. The reason why the problem of health and education continue to grow rather than reduce despite all the investment of ever greater resources is that society has developed a pathological mentality. Nine out of ten people visiting their doctors do not have a diagnosable pathology, they simply have symptoms which in all probability the doctor will only palliate with the prescription of drugs. This is equivalent to simply pushing the lid down.

From the point of view of a natural health practitioner, the symptom is the way that the body is displaying an imbalance. Simply quashing the symptoms is the equivalent to taking the red light out of the dashboard rather than dealing with the reason for its being on display.

We are concerned to analyse underlying imbalances and deal with these naturally, to enable the body to heal itself. We have hundreds of tests available to us to assess these imbalances which are not shown by any conventional pathological tests.

By the same token the symptoms of learning difficulties as displayed at school are just that – symptoms – special educational help certainly does have a value but it is also very expensive and time consuming. We have found that the Sunflower Method will often diagnose and treat many of the underlying imbalances that contribute to learning difficulties. When these have been safely treated, the children are much more receptive to what their teachers are doing for them. Their health, performance, behaviour and self esteem improve, and this improvement, in turn, has a positive knock-on effect on relationships with their families and school colleagues and also improves their future prospects.

The *ad hoc* approach which deals with the many separate symptoms of the underlying imbalances we find in these children is simply not working, despite the enormous expense that society is paying in the areas of special educational health provision, law and order, social services and so on. According to recently issued documentary, they cost society an average £1 million per child over a lifetime.

We believe the approaches being advocated by the Sunflower Trust have the potential of offering massive benefits to thousands of people. Unless this knowledge and service is readily known and available to society, society is being denied a more widely safe and effective alternative which could add great freedom and opportunity for little cost. This is why we urgently need your help to expand the availability of this service to the many children who could benefit.

Contact details
The Sunflower Trust.
Tel: 01483 531498

THE ROLE OF OSTEOPATHY FOR CHILDREN WITH LEARNING DIFFICULTIES

We may suspect that our child needs extra help in his life, be it emotional, physical or educational or all of these. Where do we turn? To various professional and other agencies; but what if someone suggests that his or her child has been helped by seeing an osteopath or a cranial osteopath? What is this and how might it help a child with learning difficulties that might in turn be associated with dyslexia, dyspraxia or an autism spectrum disorder?

Cranial osteopathy, as it is commonly known, is part of osteopathy and has been used as a form of treatment since the 1930s. What is confusing is that unlike the name implies, it does not involve only treatment on the head, but is a gentle way of treating the whole body. It is used with all age groups, but has a particular relevance for certain categories of patients because it is so gentle and non-invasive. This obviously includes infants and young people. It rather belies the sustaining rumour that all visits to an osteopath involve being tied up in knots and thrown forcibly against the wall until a few 'cracks' complement the groans of the patient!

So, how might this gentle hands-on treatment help a child with these types of problems? The simple reply is probably by helping him feel more relaxed and by undoing stress patterns that have become his 'normal' everyday posture and a part of the way he uses his body.

Even if a child is more relaxed after a treatment session, will the tensions and patterns not come back the next day? Good question.

Osteopathy is based on the restoration of health and the idea that there is a strong force intrinsic to our body physiology that wants to be healthy and wants to work as best as possible. After all, this is the spark of life, and as osteopaths we endeavour to restore this through detailed study of the way the body works and by developing the manual skills required to diagnose and sensitively to treat stress and tension. We endeavour to remove some of the obstacles, in this case patterns of physical stress and tension, to improve health in the same way that we can improve the flow of a stream by moving a dam out of its course. Whether we use medications or operations, exercises or manipulations, these methods aim to remove what is getting in the way of the body working as it is designed to. We are looking for optimum health as well as assessing the causes of ill health.

The way that this may help difficulties such as dyslexia and dyspraxia is based on the intimate relationship between physical posture and alignment and good physiological functioning of breathing and an unimpeded blood supply to the brain.

What will happen if you take your child to an osteopath? The osteopath will start by taking a case history that will include general medical information, birth history, nutritional status, family, school and environmental history and any traumatic events in the child's life. This is followed by an osteopathic physical examination in which the whole muscular and skeletal structure is examined and tested for function. Following this the findings are discussed with the parent(s) and, if appropriate, a programme of treatment is planned. If recommendation for treatment ensues following a discussion of the findings with the parent(s), then a programme of treatment is planned.

As the early identification of these problems helps them to be tackled promptly and thus more effectively, so the treatment of physical patterns and tensions also benefit from early treatment. Some of these patterns appear to be caused by difficult birth processes causing compression and strains in the head and the rest of the body. However, some children with these difficulties do not have any history of trauma. They may well have an inherited tendency to this problem but may still benefit from feeling more comfortable and being helped to optimise their potential.

It is still a pleasurable surprise to me to see how, given half a chance, our bodies will respond with better function.

Contact details
James I. Sumerfield DO
Harley Street Osteopaths
103-105 Harley Street, Suite 14, London W1G 6AJ.
Tel: 020 7935 7835
Fax: 020 7224 2448
E-mail: info@harley-street-osteopaths.co.uk

THE OTHER PATH

Health & Education Together

In many cases, children are not receiving the support that they need because they are falling between education and health.

To bring these children, indeed all children, to their potential as happy, purposeful human beings, a joint approach of Health & Education Together will be the most effective.

What we do is very simple – What happens is extremely profound

NatureKids

- Full or Part-time Home from Home Education. Learning through experience and fun.
- Ideal for Indigo[1] children who experience life in a different way, gifted and individualistic children.
- Family time in Nature for Tots to Teens.

The Other Path To Literacy

- TOP Literacy programme to easily connect the brain neurons needed for spelling, reading, writing.
- TOP Handwriting to establish a fast, easy flow that will last a lifetime.
- Effective for those with Dyslexia, Dyspraxia, ADHD.

J's story

September 2001. J, aged 6 years old, found reading, spelling and written work so excruciatingly difficult that his attention span was a few minutes, and most attempts to get him involved with academic tasks were met with screaming, crying and hiding under the table. J had been unable to tap into his intelligence, cope in school or relate to his peers. He was clumsy, frustrated, and having frequent tantrums.

J started attending Home from Home Education 2 or 3 days a week, received a full spectrum of natural therapies and followed a whole food diet avoiding the foods that gave him allergic reactions.

January 2003. J now reads on his own for pleasure. He has excellent cursive handwriting. Free writing, without the need for adult support, is slowly emerging, spellings accumulate easily each week (February

1 The Indigo Children by Lee Carroll and Jan Tober, Hay House Publishers, ISBN 1-561 70-608-6.

learned in one session), and his concentration is good for his age. He has a friend and is happily integrated into peer activity groups. He climbs confidently and enjoys physical activities. Life is joyous and purposeful.

TOP Parenting

Support sessions for exploring parenting and sharing happy activities as a group or at home.

Paths for children, teenagers, parents, teachers, adults – to be who they are and find out whom they can become.

Health Resources

A natural approach to building health and vitality, energy and enthusiasm, effective learning, positive behaviour.

Less stress, anger, sadness and scare,

More joy and fun.

Through Allergy Testing and Supplements, Natural Therapies, Pilates.

Information on therapies and treatments for Dyslexia, Dyspraxia, ADHD, Vision, Co-ordination;

Asthma, Eczema and all health problems.

Groups and discussions for parents.

Feedback from parents using our resources.

Facilitating inner resources for a creative, joyous, healthy, purposeful lifestyle.

Following the Rules for Fun.

Contact details
Felicity Evans and Colleagues.
Tel: 01727 827325
Mobile: 07711 946058
E-mail: olsandpjs@aol.com